Copyright
Information Technology
Public Policy

BOOKS IN

LIBRARY AND INFORMATION SCIENCE

A Series of Monographs and Textbooks

EDITOR

ALLEN KENT

Director, Office of Communications Programs
University of Pittsburgh
Pittsburgh, Pennsylvania

Volume 1. CLASSIFIED LIBRARY OF CONGRESS SUBJECT HEADINGS, Volume 1—CLASSIFIED LIST, edited by James G. Williams, Martha L. Manheimer, and Jay E. Daily.

Volume 2. CLASSIFIED LIBRARY OF CONGRESS SUBJECT HEADINGS, Volume 2—ALPHABETIC LIST, edited by James G. Williams, Martha L. Manheimer, and Jay E. Daily.

Volume 3. ORGANIZING NONPRINT MATERIALS, by Jay E. Daily.

Volume 4. COMPUTER-BASED CHEMICAL INFORMATION, edited by Edward McC. Arnett and Allen Kent.

Volume 5. STYLE MANUAL: A GUIDE FOR THE PREPARATION OF REPORTS AND DISSERTATIONS, by Martha L. Manheimer.

Volume 6. THE ANATOMY OF CENSORSHIP, by Jay E. Daily.

Volume 7. INFORMATION SCIENCE: SEARCH FOR IDENTITY, edited by Anthony Debons.

Volume 8. RESOURCE SHARING IN LIBRARIES: WHY • HOW • WHEN • NEXT ACTION STEPS, edited by Allen Kent.

Volume 9. READING THE RUSSIAN LANGUAGE: A GUIDE FOR LIBRARIANS AND OTHER PROFESSIONALS, by Rosalind Kent.

Volume 10. STATEWIDE COMPUTING SYSTEMS: COORDINATING ACADEMIC COMPUTER PLANNING, edited by Charles Mosmann.

Volume 11. USING THE CHEMICAL LITERATURE: A PRACTICAL GUIDE, edited by Henry M. Woodburn.

Volume 12. CATALOGING AND CLASSIFICATION: A WORKBOOK, by Martha L. Manheimer.

Volume 13. MULTI-MEDIA INDEXES, LISTS, AND REVIEW SOURCES: A BIBLIOGRAPHIC GUIDE, by Thomas L. Hart, Mary Alice Hunt, and Blanche Woolls.

Volume 14. DOCUMENT RETRIEVAL SYSTEMS: FACTORS AFFECTING SEARCH TIME, by K. Leon Montgomery.

Volume 15. LIBRARY AUTOMATION SYSTEMS, by Stephen R. Salmon.

Volume 16. BLACK LITERATURE RESOURCES: ANALYSIS AND ORGANIZATION, by Doris H. Clack.

Volume 17. COPYRIGHT—INFORMATION TECHNOLOGY—PUBLIC POLICY, Part I—COPYRIGHT—PUBLIC POLICIES, by Nicholas Henry.

Additional volumes in preparation

Copyright
Information Technology
Public Policy

Part I: COPYRIGHT - PUBLIC POLICIES

NICHOLAS HENRY

Center for Public Affairs
Arizona State University
Tempe, Arizona

MARCEL DEKKER, INC. New York and Basel

MARCEL DEKKER, INC.

270 Madison Avenue, New York, New York 10016

LIBRARY OF CONGRESS CATALOG CARD NUMBER: 74-83417

ISBN: 0-8247-6346-7

Current printing (last digit): 10 9 8 7 6 5 4 3 2 1

PRINTED IN THE UNITED STATES OF AMERICA

To Muriel

PREFACE

The social, political, and economic impact of the new information technologies is a little-known and poorly understood phenomenon. Parts I and II both attempt to address the implications of that impact. Part I considers the interrelationships among the new technologies, the information industries and professions, and public policies designed to manage the development and flow of knowledge in technoscientific cultures such as ours. Part II recounts the "politics of neopublishing," that is, the two-decade-long political struggle to revise United States copyright law in light of the emergent "neopublishing" technologies: photocopiers, microduplicators, and computer-based information storage and retrieval systems.

Both books are intended to appeal to all those interested in the relationship between knowledge and power, but particularly to those people concerned with this relationship as it is manifested in societies possessing a high level of both information and technology. Librarians, information scientists, educators, political scientists, economists, public and business administrators, as well as all who are connected with research, publishing, and authorship owe it to themselves and to their future patterns of professional productivity to become acquainted with the problems and issues discussed in these books.

I am indebted to Professors York Y. Willbern, Louis E. Lambert, and August Eberle of Indiana University for their suggestions and their support during the preparation of this manuscript. I would like to single out Professor Lynton Keith Caldwell, also of Indiana University, for his invaluable advice throughout the writing of this study. Mary Sinnock Young, May Lee, Zoe Dwyer, Betty Ann Chavez, Mary Davis, Avis Hawkins, Judy Perry, and Nancy Kinsey deserve high praise for their typing efforts and good will.

A great deal of thanks also must be accorded to those participants in the politics of neopublishing who so willingly gave their time and knowledge in helping me complete the project. To mention them all here would not be possible, but the following people deserve special mention: Thomas C. Brennan, Lee C. Burchinal, Mark Carroll, the late Verner W. Clapp, Sanford Cobb, Fred C. Cole, Margaret E. Ducey, Robert W. Frase, Abe A. Goldman, Charles F. Gosnell, Irwin Karp, Dan M. Lacy, Alan Latman, Austin J. McCaffrey, Stephen McCarthy, Peter K. Monk, Thomas A. Noble, Herman I. Orentlicher, Barbara A. Ringer, Rutherford D. Rogers, Gerald J.

Sophar, Sheldon Elliot Steinbach, Edwin C. Surrency, Howard M. Warrington, and Harold E. Wigren.

Finally, I am grateful for the patience of my wife, Muriel, and my children, Miles and Adrienne. It was they who put up with it.

Nicholas Henry

CONTENTS

Copyright
Information Technology
Public Policy

Chapter 1

KNOWLEDGE AND THE POLITY

The new technologies of knowledge are the sinews of advanced civilizations. Computers, photocopiers, microreproduction techniques, and cable television, to name a few, are as responsible as any other single phenomenon for conceiving ideas, for discoveries in science, for social and technical innovations, and for informed decision making in a polity reeling with future shock.

Yet, just as the new information technologies provide the means for intellectual creativity and improved decision making in virtually all circles of America's highly information-oriented culture, the new technologies themselves create economic, political, and social dilemmas. It is my purpose to consider the impact that new methods of handling information have had on American society, and to broach the public policy questions which have arisen as a result of that impact. In so doing, I shall review various public policies for "knowledge management," that is, policies affecting the production, dissemination, and use of information; consider the new technologies themselves, evaluate the role of copyright law in society; speculate on the future involvement of knowledge-based political systems and the role of information technology in public policy making; trace the complex history of the current copyright dispute as it relates to the new information technologies; and conclude with some policy suggestions for knowledge management.

Copyright is emphasized in these pages, but other public policies affect the origin and distribution of knowledge in society as well. It is these policies and the kinds of information they are designed to influence that we consider in this chapter. First, however, let us recall that knowledge influences public policies at least as much as public policies affect patterns of knowledge.

KNOWLEDGE FOR PUBLIC POLICIES

Knowledge is the essence of public policy making: Who has it and who lacks it determine what public policies will be. Like the new knowledge technologies themselves, new social institutions have evolved that are designed to affect how information is used at each stage of the policy making process. Our voting is influenced by political polls, and by how and when the findings of these opinion surveys are presented to us. The media, particularly television, are primary factors in any political campaign, and whole new organizations have blossomed which are designed exclusively to instruct candidates for public office on use of media.

Once in an elected office, policymakers rely on personal staffs whose major function is to transmit useful political information to them. Lobbyists for powerful and not-so-powerful interest groups legitimate their role in the political process by claiming to be nothing more than sources of information concerning certain public issues. Experts of all kinds are available to legislative committees. At the national level, legislators also can employ the recently expanded Congressional Reference Service of the Library of Congress, the General Accounting Office, and the newly created Office of Technology Assessment, among other information sources, as agencies existing specifically for and responsible only to the legislative branch.

Appointed policymakers in the public bureaucracy also have staffs and are beset by lobbyists, but their primary source of knowledge is the massive resource of the bureaucracy itself. More than any other political institution in the twentieth century, it is the public bureaucracy that determines public policy.

Bureaucracy and technology are inextricably intertwined, and the new information technologies, by providing information to decision-makers more rapidly and accurately than ever before, have enormously enhanced the power and autonomy of both bureaucracy and technology. The bureaucracy in effect has created for itself a new and vast power source: more information and more control over that information.

It is remarkable how unappreciated the significance of the bureaucracy is among America's political thinkers. It is evident from reading *The Federalist* that the country's most original contributors to the world's political literature did not anticipate the rise of the public bureaucracy, much less its institutional dominance in the public policy making process. Nor did they anticipate the fact that by the middle of the twentieth century there would be more Americans earning their livelihoods by working for the bureaucracy than there were Americans living when the Constitution was written. Less understandably, our current generation of political thinkers, those who are ensconced in the political science departments of universities and colleges, also have failed to appreciate the importance of the public bureaucracy despite its awesome magnitude, its growing administrative reliance on the techniques of social science, and its financial support of their own academic research. By way of illustration, a recent survey of five major political science journals of a nonspecialized nature revealed that only 4 percent of all the articles published during an eleven-year period between 1960 and 1970 dealt with bureaucratic politics, which was the only one of fifteen categories concerned with public bureaucracy. Moreover, the 4 percent figure appeared to be declining over time.

Is there a reason behind the disinterest in the public bureaucracy that is exhibited by the bulk of modern political thinkers? One hypothesis seems at least reasonable. That is, that the bureaucracy, as a public policy-making institution in a technological society, is antithetical to the pluralist paradigm of the democratic process originally conceived by James Madison and perpetrated by most of his intellectual progeny in political science departments. More pointedly, the Madisonian notion that the interests of the public will be best served in a democracy by the policy of compromise emerging from the contentions of interest groups (which "represent" those "publics" affected by the policy resolution) is of dubious validity in a techno-bureaucratic state. In brief, two overwhelming factors of modern culture, technology and bureaucracy, undermine what one political scientist has described as the hydraulic theory of the democratic process. The hydraulic thesis constitutes the basis of the pluralist paradigm shared by mainstream political scientists and it is apparent, given the short shrift accorded the public bureaucracy and technology assessment by political scientists as objects of study, that few scholars interested in politics are capable of denying interest-group pluralism as an apologia for how the public interest is achieved in a democracy.

Perhaps the hydraulic thesis still works (i. e., interest group compromises are indeed in the public interest) in legislative and adjudicative policy settings, and perhaps its provability in these settings accounts for why political scientists much prefer studying voting behavior, legislative committees, lobbyists, and the judicial process in contrast to bureaucratic politics. But in order to work, the hydraulic thesis by necessity rests on at least three implicit assumptions concerning the political process: (1) all publics affected by a particular policy question are aware that its resolution will affect them, (2) all affected publics have a reasonable understanding of the policy question, and (3) if the affected publics are unaware of the policy question, it is only a matter of time before they find out about it and join in the policy-making fray in order to protect their interests.

These assumptions, combined with some strictly enforced rules of the game, such as freedom of the press, provided a rational foundation on which the hydraulic thesis could be constructed as an explanation of the policymaking process in a democracy, at least in the eighteenth century. Yet, in the twentieth century, the interlaced forces of bureaucracy and technology deny these assumptions. For its part, bureaucracy denies assumptions (1) and (3). The well-documented penchant of bureaucrats for secrecy, and the mounting evidence that neither bureaucrats nor the citizenry always act on their most rational self-interest undercut the premises that people know, that people are informed, of what matters, and that they will act on what matters.

Technology denies assumption (2). Technology, or what is perceived by the people as being science applied for the rectification of their problems, is not simple. Technology is complicated, and it becomes more complicated when, as public bureaucrats are wont to do, technology is cast into the context of systems analysis in an effort to inhibit the proliferation of its socially dysfunctional side effects. Technology and its social assessment, by their very complexity, deny understanding to the people of what their problems are. Such concepts as "technocracy," "professionalism," "politics of expertise," "technipol," "systems politics," "neotic authority," and "participatory technology," represent intellectual efforts to address the enormous political problems of bureaucracy and technology not considered in the Madisonian pluralist paradigm, nor, for that matter, in the Constitution that Madison largely wrote. Yet, if democratic political processes are to be retained under the Constitution, bureaucracy and technology must be integrated into its framework, for the twin factors may be, in their essence, antithetical to democratic values.

PUBLIC POLICIES FOR KNOWLEDGE

Public policymakers have formulated a series of disjointed efforts that, perhaps unwittingly, attempt to reconcile technology, bureaucracy, and constitutional democracy. These may be categorized by public policies that have been established to finance knowledge creation, policies designed to disseminate knowledge via the new information technologies, and policies affecting secret, private, and public knowledge. While each policy was perceived as being essentially discrete at the time of its drafting, all in fact comprise an ecosystem of policies for knowledge management.

Policies for Financing Knowledge

One of the primary factors behind the data explosion is public policy for the financing of data production. The federal patron spends almost $20 billion annually on R & D projects. According to the Organization for Economic and Cultural Development (OECD) (1968) the U.S. Government financed 64 percent of all R & D projects in 1965, although it performed directly only 15 percent; industry conducted 70 percent, and universities 12 percent. The OECD estimates that the federal government spent nearly $275 million on disseminating scientific and technical information in 1967, of which $80 million was spent directly on publication (as opposed to type-written) and dissemination of information.

In 1971 alone, the U.S. Government Printing Office (GPO) sold 78 million copies of its publications for a total of $22 million, and sales have been rising steadily since its founding in 1860. By 1972, the GPO had set up seventeen of its own bookstores across the country with more such outlets planned. Internationally, the U.S. Information Agency distributes books worldwide in fifty-seven languages; by 1971, it had published and disseminated 19,220 editions totalling 157,200,000 copies. It has been stated that the federal government probably spends about $600 million annually on all types of printing, and publishes approximately 100,000 reports and 450,000 new books, articles, and papers every year.

Policies for Information Technologies

In addition to financing the production and dissemination of knowledge, the federal government also promulgates policies for the new technologies of knowledge. Notable in this regard are the numerous rulings by the Federal Communications Commission, which affect virtually all the mass media; the President's Office of Telecommunications Policy, which has influenced the affairs of a variety of information technologies from communications satellites to the political policies of the press; and the National Science Foundation, which has been instrumental in establishing computer-based information systems in a number of academic fields.

New agencies designed to influence public policies for new information technologies come and go, reflecting by their very "ad hocracy" the fast changing milieu of the knowledge technologies. For example, while the Committee on Scientific and Technical Information of the Federal Council for Science and Technology once was formally responsible for coordinating federal scientific information policies, no one today seems entirely sure about what happened to it as a result of former president Richard M. Nixon's virtual elimination of the White House science advisory agencies in 1973. Relatedly, such committees as the National Commission on Instructional Technology and the National Commission of Libraries and Information Science surface and then submerge from time to time. Proposals for new bureas equipped to deal with policies for information technologies are made, but there is no set pattern in terms of what eventually is done with these suggestions. Some drift listlessly, such as the proposed National Commission on New Technologies Uses of Copyrighted Works. The proposal, which first appeared in 1967, presently is attached to the Copyright Law Revision Bill, and has spawned a series of privately held "Parliaments on New Technological Uses of Copyrighted Works." Other notions are killed outright, such as the proposal which emerged in 1965 for a National Data Bank, or Center, and in which a number of congressmen took self-righteous glee in hacking apart over a period of two years. Still other ideas succeed, such as the enactment in 1973 of an Office of Technology Assessment, which apparently won congressional support because it was perceived as a means of offsetting the bureaucracy's near monopolization of scientific and technical information.

While the funding of information production and the creation of new policy-making bodies for new information technologies are important functions of government, the most salient kinds of public policies are those designed to affect the flow of knowledge itself. Information, of course, may assume many forms in the polity; news, propaganda, blackmail, opinions, exposés, ideas, and findings from science and social science are only some of them. In turn, informational forms may be classified along a variety of dimensions, secret and public information, personal and societal information, factual and fictional information , information that can be labelled according to particular academic disciplines, and copyrighted and uncopyrighted information. These classifications are less than neat; they overlap a great deal. For instance, copyrighted information often is public, fictional (in the sense of belles lettres), academic, and societal in character, while uncopyrighted information usually is secret, factual, and personal. Nevertheless, the major policies for knowledge management can be categorized according to three extremely broad types: secret knowledge, private knowledge, and public knowledge. These groupings relate to the breadth of dissemination that the information is permitted by the state.

Policies for Secret Knowledge

Let us first consider the primary public policies for secret knowledge. Here, of course, we have an instant problem because the policies themselves are for the most part secret, enigma wrapped in riddle, so to speak. In fact, we ought not even to speak of "public" policies because public is a misnomer in this context; policies for secret knowledge are not public but secret.

We the people do know, however, that secret knowledge is subject to a complex system of classification by the espionage establishment. How that system works is unknown, but it is thought that the James Bondish categories of "for offical use only," "classified," "confidential," "secret," "top secret," and "for your eyes only" are labels used mainly for public consumption. The real systems, and there are many, appear to be based on numbers and colors, such as "umbra," denoting the darkest part of the shadow. In these policies for secret knowledge we hear such terms as "no forn" (for no foreign distribution) and "close hold," which apply to the need to know categories, and "green door," which identifies policies dealing with S.I., or sensitive information.

Americans got a glimpse of how these systems operate when Daniel Ellsberg leaked the Pentagon Papers in 1971. Ellsberg, a RAND Corporation analyst, released more than 7,000 pages of top secret information not to the enemy, an act which provides the justification of policies for secret knowledge, but to the Senate Foreign Relations Committee, The Washington Post, and The New York Times, or, in reality, to the American people. When the United States government prosecuted Ellsberg and later hounded him, as it came out in the Watergate trials, by trying to illegally blot his personal reputation, the government was placed in the position of implying that the people were the enemy. At least the courts disagreed. But, after perusing the Pentagon Papers, there is reason to believe that the people were indeed thought to be the enemy in some circles of government. It often is this kind of knowledge, knowledge that could be embarrassing to the government or the people in it but not to the country, that is protected by secret policies.

This kind of information comprises the category of private knowledge. Obviously, if a person, such as a president, is in a position to apply policies for secret knowledge to what in actuality is only private knowledge, then he most likely will try to do so since such an act will reduce the risk of embarrassment. When we learn that the Department of Defense alone has some 20 million documents officially classified as secret, we can only speculate about the proposition on those papers actually vital to the country's security.

To limit the possibility that public officials might use policies for secret knowledge in order to hide embarrassing knowledge, Executive Order 11652 was enacted and an Interagency Classification Review Committee was established in 1972. The effect of both actions was to speed the declassification of secret information, assure a public review of secret material after ten years of its classification, automatically declassify all information after thirty years unless the relevant department head personally prohibits it, and limit the number of administrators permitted to classify top secret information. Within the first year after these measures were initiated, top secret classifiers in the federal government were reduced by 71 percent, except for the Central Intelligence Agency, which reduced them by 83 percent. Classifiers of all kinds of information were reduced by 63 percent overall.

These reductions likely are to the good. Secrecy is antithetic to innovation, regardless of whether we are considering innovations in bureaucratic or scientific decision making. Harold L. Wilensky (1967) has addressed the problems of secret knowledge in bureaucratic decision making and has concluded that secrecy is the paramount reason behind poor public policies in a democracy. Wilensky scores the organizational pathologies engendered by excessive secrecy such as the distorting effects it has on administrative communications; the protection it affords those bureaucrats who are motivated by malice; the undercutting of procedures, due process, and protection of personal liberties that is facilitated by secrecy; and the demoralizing effects of secret surveillance on organizational members. Wilensky is concerned with the intraorganizational costs of secrecy, and argues that policies for secret knowledge inhibit the formulation of effective, sensitive, and responsive public policies on a vast scale. Hence he urges that policies for secret knowledge be strictly limited and controlled.

Aside from the internal bureaucratic pathologies that stem from excessive secrecy, there also is the danger spawned by secrecy in terms of the bureaucracy's relations with its external environment. The bureaucracy's penchant for secrecy makes popular responsibility, accountability, and control supremely difficult to achieve. The remarkable German sociologist, Max Weber (Walker, 1967), addressed himself to this problem some seventy years ago: "Every bureaucracy seeks to increase the superiority of the professionally informed by keeping their knowledge and intentions secret. . . The pure interest of the bureaucracy in power, however, is efficacious far beyond those areas where purely functional interests make for secrecy. . . In facing a parliament, the bureaucracy, out of a sure power instinct, fights every attempt of the parliament to gain knowledge by means of its own experts or from interest groups."

Examples verifying Weber's statement are numerous. For instance, it is well known that agencies of the United States government leak information on a highly selective basis. The State Department granted access to its files on our intervention in the Dominican Republic to Jeremy Slater, a Latin American scholar sympathetic to that intervention, but denied access to Theodore Draper, an expert of equal merit but unsympathetic to that intervention. Similarly, when Dr. Richard Garwin's study panel on the proposed supersonic transport plane reported that the SST might imperil the atmospheric environment, Dr. Lee DuBridge, then Director of the President's Office of Science and Technology and Garwin's superior, did not permit Congressman Henry S. Reuss to read a copy of Garwin's report. DuBridge took his action on the specific instructions of former Presidential Adviser John Ehrlichman, and Reuss was able to read the report only after a two-year court fight. With hindsight, most observers agree that both these secrecy-saturated public policies, the Dominican intervention and the SST, were of low quality. The United States still is trying to regain the ground it lost in Latin American as a result of its incursion, and it is difficult to stifle a smirk over the British and French difficulties with their Concorde.

Policies for secret knowledge can exercise debilitating effects on the progress of science and the useful arts as well, at least when these policies are administered inappropriately. The renowned nuclear physicist, Edward Teller (1973), who is no friend of liberal overtures toward the Communist countries, has stated that the international secrecy enshrouding nuclear physics is a "reactionary trend" which "did not prevent the loss of leadership by the United States in the field of nuclear weapons." He added that informational barriers "are harmful to science and are a source of weakness in the free world."

The dysfunctions of secrecy in science are manifold. Fusion energy, for example, is a promising area of nuclear research that holds immense potential for alleviating the fossil fuel crunch. Yet, because of Soviet secrecy concerning their considerable progress with thermonuclear machines and American secrecy over their advances in laser-induced fusion, both of which are areas vital to the fusion energy process, no one wins and everyone loses, with the possible exception of the oil companies. Conversely, American openness regarding electronic data processing technologies, which never has been a classified field, has permitted the United States to acquire and maintain a commanding, worldwide lead in computer science.

Physicist Earl Callen (1973), has phrased the matter in particularly succinct terms.

> I have seen scientists, engineers, and mathematicians denied access to papers which they had themselves written. I have seen personnel denied jobs. . . because of differences in civilian and military security clearance standards. I have seen a good scientist denied security clearance because he testified as a character witness in a security hearing for a person who was cleared as a result of that hearing. I have seen classified papers, carefully guarded, restricted in distribution, while the same paper was freely circulated, widely known, and referenced in the open literature.

Policies for Private Knowledge

We noted earlier that a major problem of policies for secret knowledge was that they were applied all too frequently to private knowledge, that is, knowledge which is potentially embarrassing. Like secret knowledge, private knowledge demands its own kinds of policies but, unlike policies for secret knowledge, policies for private knowledge are truly public, i.e., the people may know about them, how they work, and how they fail.

Most of us are familiar with the problems of private knowledge. The concept of invasion of privacy, for example, represents a violation of private knowledge. These invasions take at least three patterns: surveillance (both criminal and political), computer-based data sharing, and the custom of executive privilege.

Technology has permitted a quantum leap in both the scope and sophistication of government surveillance of its citizens. Telephone taps, listening guns, hidden cameras, and a plethora of similar devices are all now ugly facts of American life. Indeed, American dictionaries now are being published that offer us a new English verb: to surveil. In 1974, Dr. Jerome B. Wiesner (1974), president of the Massachusetts Institute of Technology and who is likely as aware as anyone of new developments in the snooping technologies, warned a commencement audience that the "flagrant misuse of electronic surveillance devices" could succeed in dismantling democracy in America.

Most people do not mind government surveillance of criminals when that surveillance is conducted reasonably and under the constraints of due process of law. In the Nixon Administration, however, many constraints fell by the wayside. In 1969, for example, the Justice

Department, defending its wiretapping of the Chicago Eight sans such niceties as search warrants, contended that the inherent powers doctrine of the Constitution permitted the President and his officers to engage in any "intelligence-gathering operations he believes are necessary to protect the security of the nation," and added that "Congress cannot tell the President what means he may employ to obtain information he needs to determine the proper deployment of his forces." Fortunately, the trend in the judiciary has been running counter to this kind of thinking, arguing that vague regulations and casual due process can mitigate against the citizen's exercise of his constitutional rights.

The federal government gets most of its authority to eavesdrop from Title III of the Omnibus Crime Control and Safe Streets Act of 1968 which permits wiretapping by court order. Prior to 1968, only state government officials could indulge in wiretapping legally, and in that year state officials listened to 66,716 conversations. But, by 1971, at least 498,325 private conversations were recorded by government employees. In the four years since the Bill's passage 93,080 people had been spied on, but of these barely 1 percent (1,154) had been convicted of a crime.

More significantly, national security wiretaps, as opposed to criminal wiretaps, require no court orders. An investigation by Senator Edward M. Kennedy revealed that between 1969 and 1970 there were almost as many national security wiretaps as there were court-ordered wiretaps, and that the average eavesdropping period for the warrantless wiretaps was three to nine times longer than that of the court-ordered ones. Political, in contrast to criminal, surveillance would appear to be a substantial enterprise of the federal government.

Perhaps the most notorious example of the political surveillance being executed under the guise of national security is the Watergate scandal, including the illegal entry of Democratic Party headquarters, the burglary of Daniel Ellsberg's psychiatrist's office, and the Presidential cover-ups of those incidients, acts which were conceived and sponsored by White House advisers. But an equally disconcerting and more pervasive kind of political surveillance came into light in 1970. This was the revelation that, since 1965 the United States Army had been operating an extensive domestic intelligence-gathering apparatus based at Fort Holabird, Maryland. Almost 1,000 plain-clothes agents operating out of some 300 offices nationwide sent regular reports concerning the lawful political activities of all kinds of groups and individuals to CONUS (Continental United States) Intelligence Branch, Operations IV, U.S. Army Intelligent Command at Fort Holabird. There, army personnel in the Investigative Records Repository coded and stored the incoming data on an IBM 1404 according to ninety-six categories relating to incident reports (involving such happenings as domestic disturbances) and personality reports (designed to assimilate information on civilians unassociated with the military). Blacklists of politically active people and reports of political meetings were sent over a special teletype network to all army commands and were provided to other agencies that requested them. Among the organizations and individuals who had dossiers assembled in the army's computer were the National Urban League, the Young Americans for Freedom, the Southern Christian Leadership Conference, the John Birch Society, the Center for the Study of Democratic Institutions, the National Association for the Advancement of Colored People, Rear Admiral Arnold E. True, Brigadier General Hugh B. Hester (both Vietnam war critics), Senator Adlai Stevenson, III, Georgia State Representative Julian Bond, Congressman Abner Mikva, folk singers Arlo Guthrie and Joan Baez, the Reverend Jesse Jackson, and Mrs. Martin Luther King, Jr., as well as her late husband.

No one beyond the army had control over this operation which was duplicative of FBI efforts and of questionable purpose. Ultimately, Senator Sam Ervin's Subcommittee on Constitutional Rights conducted hearings on the army's political surveillance, the American Civil Liberties Union brought two court suits, NBC gave it an hour-long story on "First Tuesday," and by 1971 the army's domestic spying bureaucracy was being dismantled.

The army's surveillance program relates to another major problem of policies for private knowledge; the practice of data sharing among disparate computer systems. Among the agencies that could draw on the army's memory bands were the FBI, the Secret Service, the CIA, the National Security Agency, the Civil Service Commission, the Atomic Energy Commission, the Defense Intelligence Agency, the Navy, the Air Force, and just about any other agency remotely involved in security.

Still, such a situation is preferable to that of the private sphere where data exchanges can become pretty fast and loose. Security investigation agencies and credit companies engage most often in the practice of exchanging personal data about private citizens, and such organizations can control enormous quantities of information, both accurate and inaccurate. The largest of them, Retail Credit Company, has 7,000 investigators and files on 42 million people. Retail Credit and enterprises like it buy private files from each other and from government agencies. In the 1960s a private mortgage lender could purchase a person's confidential file (which included information on the applicant's marital stability) from the Federal Housing Administration for $1.50. Similarly, the army's notorious practice (since abandoned in 1974) of affixing all discharge papers (honorable or otherwise) with SPN (Service Performance Number) numbers, which encoded such factors as the employment suitability of the veteran for prospective employers but which were undecipherable to the veteran himself, constituted an exchange of information between systems that could plague the unwitting victim for the remainder of his life. Even the FBI's National Crime Information Center, which centralizes dossiers on individuals from local police departments all over the country, has been known to include the fact of a person's arrest or indictment but not the fact that he or she was found innocent. The Center's memory bands are open to virtually all public agencies conducting security investigations.

The major public policy for data transaction arrangements is the Fair Credit Reporting Act of 1970. This act applies to private credit and employment investigstion firms, and its principal feature is to force the organization to divulge certain kinds of data on a person in the event he demands to see his dossier. Such firms also are required to delete obsolete information from their files, which is defined as adverse information more than seven years old, such as bankruptcies and arrests.

The credit investigation companies resisted the act, arguing for voluntary self-regulation and no government interference whatever. After its passage, however, the companies reluctantly complied, but with a talent for spotting loopholes. Disclose, for example, is interpreted by most companies as meaning a verbal disclosure only, and a citizen is not permitted to actually read his own file. Sources of information and company customers buying the information are excluded by the act from these disclosures. Even so, these customers must receive permission of the applicant to make a credit check and must supply complete reports of that check in writing to the citizen within five days of receiving his or her request. The Consumer Protection Commission is charged with enforcing the act.

A policy quite different in kind from those of surveillance and data sharing also is used for private knowledge. This is the custom of executive privilege, or the withholding of information by the executive. Executive privilege, or the principle of confidentiality, is a custom because it is sanctioned neither by statutory law nor by the Constitution, unless, of course, one wishes to justify its use via the implied powers doctrine. While it is a custom that has been with us for some time, in 1794 George Washington invoked it in a minor way as President with regard to some French and American diplomatic correspondence, executive privilege as a political tool has received its real impetus only in the last two or three decades. Between 1956 and 1972 executive privilege was used at least seventeen times by four administrations. Most of these instances directly concerned foreign affairs, but the trend clearly is in the direction of applying executive privilege to informations dealing with charges of misconduct, or to the members and actions of executive departments. Jefferson invoked executive privilege relative to Aaron Burr's imperial schemes; Jackson used it in an incident involving the defrauding of the Cherokee Nation; Buchanan applied it to the landing of an illegal cargo of slaves on the Georgia coast; Lincoln used it with regard to his arrest of Brigadier General Stone; it was invoked on several occasions between 1900 and 1920 for the benefit of the Justice Department and its policies towards trusts and private companies; Truman's presidential assistant cited it in returning House subpoenas having to do with the administration of the Taft-Hartlye Act; Eisenhower employed it to deny then Senatory Lyndon B. Johnson's request for internal memoranda relating to national preparedness; Kennedy used it to avoid disclosing some National Security Council papers; and Johnson invoked it to retain documents relating to the activities and nomination of Abe Fortas as Chief Justice of the Supreme Court.

Executive privilege has been used on many other occasions as well. Former President Nixon's use of the custom in denying various congressional committees tape-recorded and written evidence pertaining to Watergate has been the most controversial use of executive privilege to date, although he had invoked the doctrine in at least four separate instances preceding Watergate as a justification for his refusal to permit congressional committees to see documents pertaining to FBI investigative files (in 1971), certain United States Information Agency policies, and the Cambodian incursion (both in 1972). It was the Nixon Administration's policy that executive privilege may be employed by any department or agency head after consulting with the Justice Department.

The policy of executive privilege, while unsanctioned by law, is perhaps the single most formidable public policy dealing with the flow of knowledge among the branches of government and the society at large. Many argue that its use has been carried to excess, but it will be up to the courts to develop guidelines governing its future applications. The 8 to 0 landmark decision by the U.S. Supreme Court in 1974 to require former President Nixon to yield certain of his taped conversation to the special prosecutor in the Watergate affair represents a genuinely promising beginning in this direction.

Policies for Public Knowledge

The final major information type that is susceptible to public policies is public knowledge. Public knowledge is information that is open to all, or should be. As with our preceding information types, dangers to the democratic process arise when policies for secret or private knowledge are designed to discourage such dysfunctions from occurring.

The principal public policy for public knowledge is, of course, our constitutional right to freedom of the press. The most recent serious challenge to freedom of the press arose in 1971 when the Nixon Administration brought suit against The Washington Post and The New York Times for publishing excerpts from the Pentagon Papers. Although the U.S. Supreme Court eventually upheld the newspapers' right to publish the excerpts, it did so on the basis of what amounted to a technicality and not on the constitutional principle of a free press.

Less pervasive but more pointed policies than that of freedom of the press are at least three laws specifically designed to keep public knowledge from becoming private knowledge: the Freedom of Information Act of 1967, the National Environmental Policy Act of 1969, and the Federal Advisory Committee Act of 1972. To those statutes we must add a fourth, the Copyright Act of 1909, which is considerably broader and more constitutional in scope than are the preceding policies.

The Freedom of Information Act waspassed by Congress in an effort to open up the federal bureaucracy to the media and consumer groups. Any citizen may receive any agency documents that he or she requests with certain specific exceptions. They are documents that have been classified as secret for reasons of national security; those relating solely to internal personnel practices; those specifically exempted by statute; those pertaining to trade secrets; agency memoranda concerning policy suggestions; medical and related files of agency personnel; and investigatory files compiled for law enforcement purposes.

The Freedom of Information Act has not met with outstanding success. Public bureaucrats have shown themselves most adept at circumventing it. Among the tactics used are (1) the contamination tactic in which potentially embarrassing unclassified information is "contaminated" by inserting classified data into the file; (2) the specificity tactic in which an agency will delay responding to requests for files on the basis that the requests were not adequately specific; (3) the search fee tactic where by the agency imposes an arbitrarily high fee for gathering the solicited information; and (4) the trade secrets tactic in which an exemption pertaining to a trade secret is extended by the agency to all other information provided by the manufacturer.

These tactics to preserve bureaucratic privacy have been effective: a requester of information can wait more than two years before all the tactics and appeals are fully played out and the case is brought to court. Of the more than 200 cases brought to court under the act by 1972, only 10 had been brought by newspapers which originally were seen as being the principal beneficiaries of the legislation. By way of indicating the failure of the act, a survey of twenty-eight leading Washington correspondents conducted in 1972 by the American Society of Newspaper Editors found that nineteen replied that government secrecy had increased, eight perceived no substantial change in governmental practices, and only one saw a decrease in levels of secrecy.

The states have been active in helping to assure the viability of the right to know. In a 1973 study of state public records laws conducted by the Freedom of Information Clearinghouse, it was found that forty-four of the fifty states have some sort of statute granting citizen access to public records, ranging from one sentence in length to laws patterned after the federal Freedom of Information Act. The Clearinghouse adjudged only fourteen of the state laws to be fully adequate, but most states are trying to improve public access to public records, and some states, such as Oregon, have improved on the federal version. Forty-one states have laws that apply both to local as well as state government records, nine have laws that apply to the legislature as well as to the executive, fifteen have laws thatpermit the courts to force full disclosure, and nineteen have penalty sections in their laws involving fines or jail sentences for public officials who are found in violation of the law.

In an effort to close some of the loopholes in the federal Freedom of Information Act, in 1972 Congress enacted the Federal Advisory Committee Act despite Nixon Administration efforts to head off its passage by Executive Order. The purpose of the act is to assure public access to the meetings of various advisory committees associated with federal agencies, since a considerable number of crucial public policies are formulated during these meetings. The act has met with some limited success, but federal bureaucrats have shown themselves adept at circumventing its intent notably, the Office of Management and Budget issued a set of guidelines designed to expedite agency disregard for the act; there exists no satisfactory means for challenging an agency head's decision to close a meeting; and agencies use the techniques of short notices, inconvenient meeting places, and similar tactics to discourage open access.

A third statute designed to assure that public knowledge remains public is in many ways broader in scope than the preceding two. This is the National Environment Policy Act, particularly Section 102. Section 102 requires all federal agencies to prepare a detailed statement concerning the potential ecological impact of all "major Federal actions significantly affecting the quality of the human environment," and to list alternative courses of action. As the President's Council on Environmental Quality (itself created by the act) has noted, this "action-forcing" provision is "without a close statutory precedent" and has provided "a mechanism for significant reform in Government decision-making." The sweeping breadth of the act is the result of two mechanisms. The first is that almost any major project undertaken by private industry today has some kind of federal involvement, either fiscal or regulative; and the second, that any citizen may file suit in court against the agency writing the impact statement on the ground that the statement is inadequate in its consideration of the environment or represents a deliberate whitewash by the agency.

While the administration of the act has met with some setbacks, notably the ultimate decision to construct the Alaskan pipeline, a number of environmentally questionable projects have been stopped or revised because of Section 102's affects on federal policy making. By mid-1973, 4,232 environmental impact statements had been filed with the Council on Environmental Quality. They were submitted by virtually every agency of the federal government, and covered such diverse enterprises as road construction, watershed protection, flood control, airport construction, navigation projects, parks, wildlife refuges, recreational facilities, electric power plant construction, pesticide and herbicide uses, forestry, and many others.

The three statutes for public knowledge that we have reviewed here appear relatively limited in their scope when compared to copyright law. While copyright in one sense, certainly, is a statute, it also is a constitutional principle. Article I, Section 8 of the Constitution states that "The Congress shall have Power . . . To promote the Progress of Science and useful Arts, by securing for limited Times to Authors . . . the exclusive Right to their respective Writings . . . " Hence, copyright, as a public policy, is almost as integral to our form of government as is freedom of the press. Moreover, it is the only public policy extant which is designed specifically to promote the creation of new concepts, ideas, and theories for society, as well as to encourage their dissemination.

The extensiveness of copyright as a public policy for public knowledge is indeed awesome. In 1968, annual copyright registrations exceeded the 300,000 mark for the first time and has been climbing steadily since. An approximate total of 10 million items were copyrighted from 1897, when the present registration system began, to 1958. Presently, there are about 6,600,000 items of intellectual property in this country that are protected by copyright. Not only are books, essays, periodicals, and poems copyrighted, but musical scores, songs, textile designs, games, maps, architectural drawings, works of art, reproductions of art, scientific drawings, illustrations, computer programs, photographs, prints, motion pictures, records, commercial prints, labels, jewelry designs, and foreign works as well. These creations may be protected from free use by copyright, whether they ever are disseminated by their owners or not, for a period as long as fifty-six years under the 1909 act.

Actually, copyright protection can extend to works never registered formally by the U.S. Copyright Office nor even covered by the current copyright act. The hazy legal area of common law copyright protects materials not published. Common law copyright usually is though of as extending to manuscripts, but it can extend to other creations as well until they are published, in which event statutory law applies.

What constitutes publication is vital to common law copyright, and is a point that remains unsettled. Making copies freely available is considered to be unequivocal general publication, and is protected by statute. But when a writer circulates a limited number of copies for a specific purpose, it is called "limited publication." Limited publication is protected by common law copyright. Copyright of some variety would appear to affect virtually every intellectual creation in the United States that is produced in a tangible format.

In fact, there is reason to believe that copyright could be extended to intangible formats. In Denmark and Sweden, readers who borrow books from public libraries pay a toll to copyright owners for the act of reading their works. The rationale behind this public lending right is that small populations and languages of restricted use necessitate an additional means of support for copyright owners. Nevertheless, recent developments in the United Kingdom and in this country indicate the predisposition of English-speaking copyright owners for a general lending right or a binding right. The appearance in books of versos which state that the volume is not to be "lent, resold, hired out or otherwise circulated" in any other than its present binding without the consent of the publisher, attests to such an attitude on the part of copyright proprietors.

Because of its pervasiveness, copyright expresses a policy not only for public knowledge, but also constitutes a public policy for research, social innovation, and the right of citizens to own property, in this instance, intellectual property. Knowledge, research, innovation, and property are topics of some consequence in any society.

IS PUBLIC KNOWLEDGE MORE IMPORTANT THAN SECRET AND PRIVATE KNOWLEDGE?

Copyright applies to more public knowledge than any other public policy with the possible exception of freedom of the press. Some might say so what, and argue that it is the information used by policymakers in their most secret sessions which really matters, the knowledge that is useful precisely because few people have access to it.

It can be argued, perhaps, that copyrighted information is considerably less crucial to the political process than the uncopyrighted, secret, or private knowledge that we, the public, seldom see. I would disagree. No doubt, secret knowledge has swayed political decisions radically. But even these decisions must be made in a milieu which is saturated by information that is read, heard, or seen by the public at large, or by various publics peculiarly pertinent to a particular political issue.

From another perspective, the uses of private, uncopyrighted knowledge are questions of greater immediacy to the individual citizen in this country than are questions involving accessible, copyrighted information. Clumsy political surveillance and irresponsible credit checks are facts of American life that affect us all at the most personal levels.

In the long run, however, information that is designed to transmit ideas is the kind of knowledge that invariably is associated with social progress. This is true no matter how progress is defined, whether as the attainment of industrial growth, of environmental preservation, or of spiritual fulfillment. Information, after all, is what changes us. The kind of information that changes society, that is, education, scientific, and social scientific knowledge, generally is subject to copyright law.

Moreover, developments in the technology of information dissemination and access would seem to indicate that public information (as identified by its copyright status) will become increasingly significant in public policy making. While knowledge was always power, today it is the central and controlling force in society, and the pivotal value and indispensable resource in public policy formulation. This new dimension of knowledge has made academics and universities, which deal almost exclusively in publicly accessible and copyrighted information, far more powerful in terms of social development than industrialists and generals, factories and armies. In an age in which biologists discuss the possibility of "cloning" twenty-three Toscaninis (or half-a-dozen Hitlers) through new discoveries in genetics, and in which popular magazines tell us how to build a nuclear bomb in terminology readily comprehensible by any nine-year-old, such a viewpoint does not seem at all far-fetched. Nor by implication, does the hypothesis that the copyrighted information on which academicians and the rest of the public chiefly rely for developing their scientific, political, and social perspectives, is at least as vital to the political process as secret and uncopyrighted knowledge, seem unreasonable. After all, 98.9 percent of all American homes with electricity have at least one television set, and 50 to 60 percent of Americans rely on television as their chief news source; nine out of ten American adults read a newspaper every day; and more than three-quarters of American adults can recall some item relating to science or medicine that they read, heard, or saw via the media. Copyright affects all these sources of public knowledge. Other than freedom of the press, no other public policy nor any public agency can make such a claim.

In this chapter we have reviewed some major public policies for financing knowledge, knowledge technologies, secret knowledge, private knowledge, and public knowledge, in an effort to place copyright law in its proper context. The remainder of this book concerns copyright and the principal challenges to its continuation as a policy for the origination and dissemination of knowledge in society, i.e., the new information technologies. We consider these new technologies in the next chapter.

REFERENCES

Beer, Stafford (1970). "Managing Modern Complexity." The management of information and knowledge. A compilation of papers prepared for the Eleventh Meeting of the Panel on Science and Technology, Committee on Science and Astronautics, U.S. House of Representatives. Washington: U.S. Government Printing Office.

Boulding, Kenneth (1964). The meaning of the twentieth century: The great transition. New York: Harper and Row, Publishers.

Buckingham, Walter (1966). The coming victory over paper. In Public administration: Readings in institutions, processes, behavior, 1st ed. Robert, T. Golembiewski, Frank Gibson, and Geoffrey Y. Cornog (Eds.). Chicago: Rand McNally and Company, 63-65.

Caldwell, Lynton K. (1967). Managing the scientific super-culture: The task of educational preparation. Public Administration Review XXVII, June, 128-133.

Callen, Earl (1973). "Statement." Executive privilege, secrecy in government, freedom of information. Hearings before Subcommittees on Government Operations and the Judiciary, U.S. Senate, 93rd Cong., 1st Sess. on S. 858, S. Con. Res. 30, S. J. Res. 72, S. 1106, S. 1142, S. 1520, S. 1927, and S. 2073. April 10-12; May 8-10, 16. Vol. 1. Washington: U.S. Government Printing Office, 298-308.

Carroll, James D. (1969). Noetic authority. Public Administration Review XXIX, September/October, 492-500.

Carroll, James D. (1971). Participatory technology. Science CLXXI, February 19, 647-653.

Council on Environmental Quality (1973). "Environmental Quality— 1972: Third Annual Report." Washington: U.S. Government Printing Office.

de Solla Price, Derek J. (1963). Little science, big science. New York: Columbia University Press.

de Solla Price, Derek J. (1967). Networks of scientific papers. In The growth of knowledge: Readings on organization and retrieval of information, Manfred Kochen (Ed.). New York: John Wiley and Sons, Inc., 145-155.

Ellul, Jacques (1967). The technological society. New York: Alfred A. Knopf.

Gipe, George A. (1967). Nearer to the dust: Copyright and the machine. Baltimore: Williams and Wilkins Press.

Glasser, Ira and Schwartz, Herman (1972). Your phone is a party line. Harper's Magazine, October, 106-108, 111-114.

Katz, Aaron (1964). Toward high information level culture. Cybernetica VII, No. 3, 203-245.

Lane, Robert E. (1966). The decline of politics and ideology in a knowledgeable society. American Sociological Review XXXI, October, 649-662.

London, Gertrude (1968). The publication inflation. American Documentation XIX, April, 137-141.

Meynaud, Jean (1968). Technocracy. London: Faber and Faber.

Organization for Economic Cooperation and Development (1968). Reviews of National Science Policy: United States, 34. Paris: OECD.

Platt, John Rader (1966). The step to man. New York: John Wiley and Sons.

Teller, Edward (1973). "The Freedom of Scientific Information." Executive Privilege, Secrecy in Government, Freedom of Information. Hearings before Subcommittees of the Committees on Government Operations and the Judiciary, U.S. Senate, 93rd Cong., 1st Sess. on S. 858, S. Con. Res. 30, S. J. Res. 72, S. 1106, S. 1142, S. 1520, S. 1927, and S. 2073. April 10-12; May 8-10, 16. Vol. 1. Washington: U.S. Government Printing Office, 304.

Peters, Charles and Branch, Taylor (1972). The case of Christopher Pyle. Blowing the whistle: Dissent in the public interest, Charles Peters and Taylor Branch (Eds.). New York: Praeger, 43-76.

Walker, Jack L. (1972). Brother Can You Paradigm? PS 5, Fall, 419-422. From Max Weber: Essays in sociology (1947), Hans H. Gerth and C. Wright Mills (Eds.). New York: Oxford University Press.

Wiesner, Jerome B. (1974). Commencement address. June 2, Cambridge: Massachusetts Institute of Technology.

Wilensky, Harold L. (1967). Organizational intelligence: Knowledge and policy in government and industry. New York: Basic Books.

Woodward, F. Peter (1967). Sounder thinking through clearer writing. Science CLVI, May 12, 743-745.

Zeigler, Harmon (1964). Interest groups in American society. Englewood Cliffs, New Jersey: Prentice-Hall, Inc.

Chapter 2

TECHNOLOGIES FOR KNOWLEDGE

In the preceding chapter we considered how knowledge affected the formation of public policies, and noted that either too many or too few data were equally dysfunctional to sound policy making. These phenomena, being swamped by data or having large gaps in needed knowledge, affect us all since all people make decisions, and always have made decisions, on the basis of information.

What is now new under the sun are technologies that enable us to reduce the dysfunctions of too many data and too little knowledge. In theory at least, more effective, focused, responsive, and parsimonious decision making results when we are presented only with data that are relevant to us and to the decision question. Information theorist Stafford Beer has cast the notion of having the right data for the right social problem in physical terms. Beer argues that today American society has "wildly overreactive reflexes" in terms of response to informational stimuli. Our data supply far exceeds our metabolic capacity to use it and to comprehend it. Beer compares this social situation to the physiological condition of clonus, i. e., we are in a "spastic society because of clonic response" which probably will get worse. He contends that the drastic refinement of massive data overload enabled by technology should reduce clonus in our culture because society's informational needs "are precisely the requirements of systemic equilibria."

THE KNOWLEDGE VERSUS DATA DILEMMA

Beer's ideas on the social pathologies engendered by too many data lead into the very useful distinction that he draws between what are "data" and what is "knowledge." Knowledge, or information, is what changes us. This distinguishes knowledge from mere data, which are cognitive stimuli that do not change us.

Because no organism, such as a political decisionmaker, can absorb and use an unlimited quantity of stimuli, there are considerably more data bouncing around in society than there is information. What is knowledge and what are data, then, is a distinction determined by the individual himself. "Meaning" and "nonsense" are relative terms; what is profound to one is poppycock to another.

The problem confronting techno-bureaucratic cultures is one of how to get relevant data to the right people since only relevancy can convert data into knowledge and hence induce change. This is a tough problem, for an integral characteristic of techno-bureaucratic states is the magnitude of data in it. Too many data swamp us, and therefore produce precisely the same dysfunctions as too little knowledge.

Estimates of the data explosion's dimensions vary, but observers generally agree that its growth is exponential. George A. Gipe notes that the first doubling of the volume of printed knowledge occurred in 1750, the second in 1900, the third in 1950, and the fourth in 1960. He adds that information was doubling at a rate of every seven years in the 1960s. John Rader Platt offers a somewhat more conservative estimate, stating that knowledge doubles approximately every generation. Derek J. de Solla Price has observed that "the body of world literature has been growing exponentially for a few centuries, and probably will continue at its present rate of growth of about seven percent per annum . . . " More in accordance with this estimate, Gipe has noted that world publishing doubles its titles every forty years, and he cites a 1960 UNESCO report which states that there are from 250,000 to 1 million volumes published each year throughout the world. American publishing doubles its output every twenty years.

Much of this bulk appears to be attributable to the phenomenal growth of science. Price was the first scholar to notice that from 80 to 90 percent of all scientists ever born are living today. Less well known is that the number of living scientists doubles every fifteen years. This expansion has resulted in the founding of 50,000 scientific periodicals (not to mention the upsurge in scientific books), 30,000 of which are still published. A total of 6 million scientific papers have been published, and it is calculated that approximately one-half million new papers will be published each year. Price notes that every scientific paper ever published is cited approximately once a year.

Regardless of its source, however, it is evidence that the data explosion has had profound effects on society. In the United States for example, paper-handling jobs have been growing dramatically while other kinds of employment have declined. In 1900, only one American worker in forty was a clerk; by 1930, this ratio was one-in-twelve; today, one of seven United States laborers is a clerk. In the 1950s, the clerical work force increased 52 percent, while the number of production workers remained about constant. Today, there are approximately two-thirds as many clerks as factory workers, and 50 percent more clerks than farmers. In this light, United States paper consumption has increased from about 60 pounds per person in 1900 to more than 400 pounds today.

Economically, the impact of information has also been profound. Both the "copyright industry" (i.e., newspaper, book, and periodical publishers, printers, photographers, media merchants, and so forth), and the "knowledge industry" (i.e., education, media, information services, research and development, and information machines), carry a heavy weight in the national economy. Although there is considerable definitional overlap in the components of the two industries, one financial analyst places the copyright industry ahead of banking, mining, and utilities in terms of contribution to the national income, and another estimates that the knowledge industry constituted 33 percent of the gross national product in 1968, or $195 (up from 26 percent, or $136 billion, in 1958). Economist E. F. Denison states that 23 percent of U.S. economic growth from 1929 to 1957 is attributable to increases in educational levels alone, and another 20 percent to advances in knowledge. When these figures are cast in terms of economic growth per person employed, 41 percent, or the largest single factor of American expansion can be attributed to improvements in education and 36 percent to advances in knowledge. The information industry is not only the fiscal foundation of the American techno-structure, but it is usurping quite a few of the floors at ground level as well.

Despite its impact, information (much less wisdom) has not been a benefit that humanity has yet derived from the flood of data currently inundating society. Sir Lindor Brown in his keynote address at the 1958 International Conference for Scientific Information in Washington, D.C., states, "There can be no doubt in the mind of anyone dealing with scientific literature that much need never be produced and of that which justifies its appearance, 80 percent could be improved by drastic reduction in length and by clear writing."

Why does this excess exist? The reason most often cited is the ecnomic and career motivations of the data-producers. Appointments and promotions frequently are determined by the quantity rather than the quality of the published work. A seldom-mentioned incentive that fosters the overproduction of data may stem from continuing reverence for the printed word, a respect which, in the words of Gertrude London, "nourishes the deep-seated vanity of some authors who like to publish because the printed word promises a kind of archival immortality . . . "

If the effects of the information are psychologically beneficial for some individual writers who contribute to its bulk, the social costs of unorganized ideas and discoveries in a scientific superculture are profound. The dysfunctions of gagging communications channels with informational overload have been noted by a number of scholars in a number of contexts. Gipe indicates the immediately measurable costs of too much information with a few selected examples:

> Recently a major United States company, working under a federal contract, spent more than $250,000 and 5 years of research in an attempt to solve an electronic switching problem important to military communications. Eventually the team of top notch mathematicians doing the research found the solution. They also discovered that the solution was available in a manuscript that had been written six months before the research project started.
>
> A cloud-seeding experiment was recently carried out at a cost of $3 million, but shortly after completion of the experiment, it was discovered that the same work had been done at an earlier date for only $256,000.
>
> In one of the nation's ballistic missile programs, a special valve was needed to solve a tricky field handling problem. After several months of intensive research, the solution was realized. In addition, it was discovered that the information on the valve existed before research started.
>
> Eighteen million dollars worth of duplicated effort came to light as the result of a discovery that two government agencies had been working on the same type of missle for over a year.
>
> And one leading manufacturing firm paid more than $8 million for the invention of a product before it realized someone else had already developed the same product.

There are also more personal liabilities associated with the knowledge explosion. It may be that the dulling effects of writing have oversaturated our minds and that we are gradually losing the ability to read with critical attention. A study by F. Peter Woodward indicated that science students experienced a measurable decline in the ability to write clearly and directly, and that their power of reading and understanding texts deteriorated markedly after the first two years in graduate schools.

There are those who cry that the information gusher must be stopped. Platt has shown the hopelessness of trying to comprehend a fraction of the world's information. He calculates that one man can "absorb" approximately 160 books annually in "a very bookish lifetime," or about 8,000 books in fifty years of diligent reading. If the totality of humanity's printed knowledge could be reduced to 10,000 pages, Platt reasons, 8,000 books would add up to four of these "microprinted sheets." The greatest of the earth's philosophers (e.g., Socrates, Kant), "universal men," (e.g., Bacon, Leonardo, Goethe), and even the encyclopedists (e.g., Aristotle, Diderot) "probably fell short in reading their 8,000 books; they were too busy thinking." It is a small wonder that John Wilkinson has estimated that the average scientific paper is read by about 1.3 people, and many are read by no one but their authors and editors.

Despite the dysfunctions of informational overload, however, librarians still are confronted with organizing the expanding volume of knowledge. In this sense, librarians feel the brunt of the information explosion. In 1831, American libraries held an average of 7,000 titles; by the 1930s, this figure was 128,000. The ten university libraries founded in 1876 in the United States held an average collection of 14,500 titles; by the 1920s their collection had grown to an average of 753,000 titles. Research libraries are essentially a twentieth century response to the information explosion. In 1900, there were less than 30 such institutions in the United States; sixty years later, this number had surpassed 10,000. A study of fifty-eight research libraries in this country indicated that they averaged yearly acquisitions of roughly 35,000 volumes in 1959-1961, a figure that doubled by 1963-1964, and which may exceed 200,000 titles by 1980, when the averaged expenditures of libraries has been estimated to be $5.4 million. The Library of Congress acquires approximately 300,000 titles each year, and twenty years ago it was calculated that research libraries were doubling in size every sixteen years.

In sum then, the data explosion not only is on us but is inundating us. It is the new information technologies that offer relief, and which largely permit the discarding of data, the gathering of knowledge, and the reducing of social clonus. The primary new knowledge technologies are photocopying, microreproduction, computer-based information storage and retrieval systems, and cable television. These are the technologies of information access. Two basic varieties of information access exist: Bibliographic (ways of locating data) and physical (ways of acquiring data for use). In this chapter we consider some social implications of these bibliographic and physical information acess technologies and conclude with some thoughts on the future development of combined information and communications technologies. Information technology is homogenizing. Recently, C. Peter McColough, president of Xerox, referred to the phenomenon in an interview. "Xerox and IBM are the two big companies exclusively in the information business . . . IBM owns the manipulative data processing part, and we own the part that puts things on paper. But the lines of separation are blurred, and it will be harder and harder to distinguish them."

Information technology has had a long history. John Rader Platt notes that vellum books appeared 2,000 years ago but only after an even longer period of technical development from ink on papyrus scolls, cuneiform scratched on clay tablets with a stylus, and hieroglyphs carved into stone with a chisel. Printing with movable type appeared only 500 years ago. What is unique today is that we are experiencing a quantum leap in the variety of ways in which information can be formed, reassembled, and distributed. Photocopying is one such way.

PHOTODUPLICATION

Making copies of copyrighted works via photography was practiced before the beginning of this century. One scholar has noted that "in its new building opened in 1897 the Library of Congress provided photographic facilities for its users." By 1911, the National Agricultural Library was supplying typewritten or photographic copies of articles on interlibrary loan, when it was inconvenient to mail original volumes. In 1900, the photostat camera was invented, sharply reducing technical complexities of the copying process, and in 1912 it was introduced by libraries as a new service for patrons.

The first xerographic photocopy was made by Chester Carlson on October 22, 1938, in Astoria, New York. By the late 1940s, two reprographic processes were in common, if relatively limited, use: photostating, which is characterized by heavy equipment and requires some technical expertise; and microfilming, which necessitates expensive viewing equipment. With the year 1950, a turning point in photocopying technology was reached; diffusion-transfer-reversal process (DTR), the thermographic process, and the xerographic process all became available in the United States. In 1952, American Photocopy introduced the first DTR machine in this country. Later that same year, Eastman Kodak announced a new process, Verifax, and a machine to accompany it, while Minnesota Mining and Manufacturing Company (3-M) backed its Thermofax, the company's tradename for a thermographic copier.

Xerox Corporation was pinning its hopes on Carlson's xerography, an electrostatic technique that ultimately would prove superior to the other processes. Xerox had acquired the basic technique from the Batelle Memorial Institute in 1948, and produced its first copier in 1950. After a decade of competing with other companies on a fairly evenly matched basis, Xerox began taking the lion's share of sales in 1960 with the introduction of its Xerox 914 copier.

The Xerox 914 was hardly the cheapest machine on the market. George A. Gipe states that the 914 costs $2,400 to manufacture, and sold for $29,500 in 1967; on a rental basis (an arrangement preferred by Xerox), it returns approximately $4,500 annually. An article in Business Week differed somewhat, saying that "some analysts estimate that copiers like the old 914 averaged close to $4,000 per year" in rent returns, a sum that "is perhaps twice the copier's cost." But the market strength of the Xerox 914 lay in its simplicity. Unlike most of its competitors, anyone could operate it. Sheets did not have to be peeled apart, liquids did not have to be applied to the negatives, exposures did not have to be set, gas did not have to be vented, pages did not have to be unbound from books and magazines, and lighting did not have to be subdued.

The 914, and three years later, the desk-top 813, were instrumental in making Xerox Corporation dominant in the copier market. Xerox had $1.4 billion in revenues in 1969, compared to $40 million in 1960. Xerox now controls at least one-third and possibly two-thirds of the photocopying market, in an industry that has thirty-six other firms manufacturing copiers.

Another significant technical development of the 1960s was the introduction of the coin-operated copier. Documat, Inc., introduced its Docustat, the first model on the market. The tone of the following quotation, written in the mid-1960s by William R. Hawken recalls the original novelty of publishing for a quarter. "The Docustat was designed from the ground up to be, of all things, a vending machine, like coffee machines, cigarette machines, or candy machines." The coin-operated copier freed numerous libraries from large capital outlays, yet still permitted the presence of a device on the premises that provided a great convenience in terms of physical access. Photostat cameras cost several thousand dollars, and only major libraries could afford them. Now virtually any lending room could afford to rent a maintenance-free photocopier.

A third photocopying development holds great potential for the many proposed and emerging information systems now dotting the United States. Facsimile transmission, a technology that permits photocopies to be exchanged between distant points via telephone connection, has been commercially available since the late 1960s. Title III of the Library Services and Construction Act encourages the integrated use of library materials, and has resulted in a number of independent empirical studies that have examined, among others, the field performance of the Xerox Magnavox Telecopier, the Xerox LDX, the Datafax 1824, the Dial/Datafax, and the Alden II Docufax.

The investigations were sponsored by a variety of library and university systems and reveal mixed reactions concerning the quality of copy resolutions, unit cost, and machine reliability. Nevertheless, they are consistent in their conclusions that facsimile reproduction would be inappropriate for their particular situations, despite testing in disparate regions of the nation and in networks ranging from fifteen to two libraries. While such findings may be momentarily discouraging to visionaries of information-sharing schemes, they have not slowed planning for such networks. And the future refinement of facsimile transmission technology seems more than likely. Librarian John Emmett Burke has argued that while "facsimile transmission has not been perfected to the point where it is feasible and economical, it must be admitted that it offers another avenue of cooperation that has implications for the acquisition policies of colleges and universities."

New developments in photocopying machinery appear every year. Of the twenty duplicators, copiers, and printers in the Xerox line, some can make imprints eighteen inches wide and as long as the role of paper used; others can be equipped with accessories that let copiers automatically feed themselves, then slit, perforate, and even collate the copies; still others are microfilm printers that can expand or contract the size of the originals. Xerox's latest machine "appears to have overskill potential," to quote one business magazine. The Xerox 4000 produces 2,700 copies of noticeably improved quality every hour. It is quiet, compact, and prints both sides of the paper automatically. As with all Xerox models, the 4000 does not require specially treated paper for its copies; only three other firms produce machines that also reproduce on any grade of paper: 3-M, Frieden, and International Business Machines (IBM). Evidently, the Xerox 4000 does not bind copies into book form, but that appears to be its sole deficiency as a neopublishing instrument. Other developments worth noting are the A-M Copier-Duplicator and A. B. Dick's System 9000, which use an electrostatically imaged master to turn out copies at extremely high speeds (the A-M model prints 5,400 copies per hour).

Such developments signify a continuance of the photocopying industry's incredibly rapid growth rate. Not long ago, photocopying was a specialized skill used by relatively few. In 1954, William R. Hawken wrote an article on "New Methods for Photocopying," in which twelve machines were described, and later said that "This was thought to be pretty good coverage for its time." Nine years later, Administrative Management contained an article that surveyed 174 copying machines. Photocopying today is a multibillion dollar concern that seems likely to continue growing and homogenizing with other information technologies.

MICROREPRODUCTION

Microreproduction, like photoduplication, is a rapidly developing technology of physical information access. But it has yet to expand and prosper in the same manner as the photocopying industry. Nevertheless, the market potential of microreproduction is immense.

Microreproduction has a dual potentiality. On the one hand, it can provide the user with a copy, either on a screen, on microfilm, or on paper. The Council on Library Resources has long been interested in developing this aspect of the microform, devoting a sixth of its budget to microreproduction over the years. Currently, however, private corporations increasingly are immersed in the technology, and today there are more than 200 different readers and reader/printers for microfiche on the market.

On the other hand, microreproduction holds out the possibility of an "ultramicro-universalium" for every man, i.e., the complete record of the world's written knowledge conveniently kept in a drawer. Platt contends that it is theoretically possible to store all of man's recorded knowledge "inside the head of a single pin . . . Hard to get at, perhaps, but what a pin!" More realistically, it is now possible with present methods to photocopy all the earth's recorded information (approximately 20 million volumes) with an optical-microscope, and to reduce its bulk to twenty volumes that would total 10,000 micro-pages; this would be the equivalent of a modern set of encyclopedias. A home-based, desk-top universal library that flashed desired information on the homeowner's television screen, and which served at least 200,000 clients, probably would sell from $3,000 to $6,000, including copyright costs.

Even if such speculation as the preceding should prove ephemeral, it is still noteworthy that libraries and other institutions of learning stand only to gain from microform technologies. It is doubtful that books and browsing through books will be displaced completely by the plastic film strip, card, and microdot. But microfirms offer insurance; the library always will have a mastercopy despite vandalism, fires, loss, and theft.

Microforms also offer the immense allure of expanding library collections at a fraction of present-day costs. Gipe estimated in 1967 that by 1970 major university research libraries would have to build "an additional 5 miles of shelf space just to hold the new volumes," if current publication rates continued. Microforms obviate these kinds of expenses.

Finally, microforms hold a tremendous potentiality for reducing the costs and speeding the distribution of information found in specialized journals. Any journal editor with a circulation of less than 50,000 will find it far cheaper to publish on microforms rather than on paper, a commodity, incidentally, that is in short enough supply as it is. These savings in production costs can be transferred to upgrading dissemination services; first-class mail can be used instead of using second-class mail. Subscription prices also can be lowered, thus off-setting the initial investment cost to the subscriber of purchasing a microfiche reader, which presently costs about half the price of a typewriter.

The realization of microduplication's potentialities has been delayed in part because cumbersome and expensive viewing equipment is required to read microforms. Hawken has stated that this technological lag likens the modern scholar to his medieval predecessor by chaining him to his source and requiring that he record his findings "by the most ancient method of all-manual transcription." Burke, too, has scored "the failure of the market to produce a small, inexpensive reader that scholars and graduate students could place beside their typewriters for immediate and daily use."

This situation may change. The United States Office of Education (USOE) recently sponsored a Microfiche Reader Conference, which set forth requirements for a microfiche reader to sell for under $50. Largely as a result of a USOE grant, DASA Corporation announced its PMR-50 reader, which will sell for $50 in quantity, and $75 in single orders.

Even more versatile technologies are developing which combine photocopying and microfilming techniques. The National Technical Information Service has a new machine (developed by Xerox Corporation) that automatically enlarges and produces paper copies of each page in the proper sequence from microfiche. Hence, the user need not rely on a microfiche reader in obtaining copies of microfiched publications.

A less prominent if highly related factor that appears to hamper the popularity of microforms is the reluctance of some scholars to use them. Burke notes that some researchers believe microfilm reading to be "tiresome and difficult," and that the "referring back process is inconvenient."

This, too, may change. Max V. Mathews and W. Stanley Brown, of the American Council of Learned Societies' Committee on Research Libraries, admit that there "is undoubtedly reader resistance," but contend that some of this reluctance may be attributable to a scholarly generation gap which may dissipate over time, "there is some evidence that the established scholar is more insistent of the original than the graduate student, and the high school students are the microfilm's warmest friends." But the real deficiency, in their view, echoes the opinions of Burke and Hawken. That is, the lack of an overall system which is engineered for the reader, a system for which the components already are designed, and "could be created with a little well-directed encouragement of existing companies plus a little standardization."

Perhaps the most significant blockage to the widespread adoption of microform systems, however, is the subject of this book: copyright law. A hypothetical microform system that permitted the copyright user to take home microcopies, as he now takes home photocopies, has all the characteristics of the present photocopying situation plus the added features of greater convenience of storage and access. Additionally, it would have far more profound effects on libraries than photocopying now does have, or probably will have.

The technology for such a microcopying system does not yet exist. But neither does it seem too far in the future.

COMPUTER-BASED INFORMATION STORAGE AND RETRIEVAL SYSTEMS AND THE RISE OF THE NETWORK

Integral to microcopying technologies are the emergence of the computer system and the computer network. What is new is the unmistakable recognition—bordering on the inevitable—that networks are finally practical and here to stay.

The notion of an information system is not new. Attempts to bring together all knowledge can be traced as far back as the ancient library at Alexandria, Sir Francis Bacon's Novum Organum, and the original Encyclopedias. Later, scholars of Great Britain's Royal Society tried (and failed) to construct a comprehensive Index of Scientific Literature and a Concilium Bibliographicum, which was an immense card index that eventually got quite out of hand and drowned in an ocean of information bits.

These forays took place prior to the advent of computers, and computers make workable information systems possible. The computer is a new tool, but its potentialities are being realized rapidly, particularly in terms of what it can mean for bibliographic access. The Ad Hoc Task Group on Legal Aspects Involved in National Information Systems of the Committee of Scientific and Technical Information Federal Council for Science and Technology, reports that there were 1,303 R & D projects on information science and technology underway in 1967, and the National Science Foundation tallied 102 projects in information coding and indexing, 126 in information retrieving systems, and 56 in the analysis and evaluation of information. Most of these projects related directly to the use of computers, and many were experimenting with machines that stored not only abstracts of articles but also whole texts. Even as these projects were being constructed, the National Science Foundation reported that at least 118 computerized information storage and retrieval systems were in operation in 1967; the Department of Defense alone had 33 of them. Similarly, computer/communications systems had grown from a paltry 31 in 1960 to more than 2,300 on-line systems in use by 1966. IBM officials have reported that more than 50 percent of all computer installations will have a communications capability by 1978.

By 1974, there were an estimated 70,000 computers manipulating data in the United States. These 70,000-odd operations largely were and are autonomous, but it apparent that rising technological, economic, and organizational pressures are giving rise to a new phenomenon in the operation of computer centers: networking.

Networking is the electronic linking-up of various computer centers in a region in order that computers may be run more economically and that users may be offered a wider variety of services. At least four technological developments have fostered the beginning of networking: the rise of ever-more-powerful but cheaper "minicomputers"; the use of computers on a remote, time-sharing basis; improvements in a number of communications technologies, notably cable television and microwave transmission; and the evolvement of large-scale, inexpensive, and low-maintenance memory banks.

Eonomic constraints also are encouraging networking. Education, which spends about $600 million in computer-related operating expenses every year, is by necessity tightening its belt in the 1970s. University computer centers are being asked to provide increasingly wide and disparate services to users while simultaneously their funding sources slowly dry up. Add to this the fact that hardware costs per computational operation are declining radically.

According to the Stanford Research Institute, the cost for the same computational function has been falling at the phenomenal rate of approximately 25 percent annually, a rate that likely will continue for the next ten years. General Electric executives have stated that the average cost of 100,000 multiplications on a computer initially was $1, had reached 25 cents by 1963-1964, and should be a nickel "in the near future."

While these plummeting hardware costs are encouraging, another computer expense has been steadily rising: software. More than 100,000 programmers earning considerably more than $1 billion in salaries a year work in the United States, and the costs of these programmers to computer users have been rising without let-up. These expenses, of course, must be considered as an integral part of the computer's overall cost, and possibly may negate declining computational costs.

It is not surprising, then, that education has been on the forefront of explaining the potentialities of computer networking, which, as a managerial system, exploits the falling hardware costs and resists the rising software costs of computer operations. The National Science Foundation has financed approximately thirty regional computer networks among colleges and universities during the 1970s, and additional interinstitutional networks have developed or are developing among university computer centers in North Carolina, Michigan, Pennsylvania, California, Missouri, New York, Minnesota, Illinois, New Jersey, Oregon, and Florida.

Perhaps the most ambitious, privately operated information system-cum-network is the Interuniversity Communications Council, or EDUCOM. Strictly defined, EDUCOM is not an information system, but a vehicle for collaboration in utilizing the emerging equipment and techniques that are revolutionizing the handling of knowledge. Eight charter members founded EDUCOM in 1964 with a $750,000 grant from the Kellogg Foundation, and in 1969 it had 102 member institutions and organizations. The purpose of this suprauniversity organization is to foster an information network, unrestricted by geographic or time constraints, that would, to quote an EDUCOM official, "make material in many forms almost instantly available to scholars wherever on the continent they might be." EDUCOM's proponents envision typewriter-like terminals in home and office that permit information exchanges by voice, television screen, and long-distance xerography. EDUCOM's most notable accomplishments thus far are its major Summer Study on Information Networks of 1966, a series of networking conferences held between 1972 and 1973 that were sponsored by the National Science Foundation, and the development in 1974 of a Planning Council on Computing in Education and Research, comprised of senior university administrators and computer specialists from a number of different institutions.

EDUCOM officials are aware that beyond "any technical difficulties, the electronic exchange of knowledge is fraught . . . with political and sociological implications, not the least complex of which is the copyright problem."

It was precisely this operation that led Williams & Wilkins Company, a publisher in the biomedical field, to file suit in the United States Court of Claims against the National Library of Medicine, (NLM) and the National Institutes of Health.

The Educational Resources Information Center (ERIC), operated by the United States Office of Education, is even more comprehensive than the Medical Library Analysis and Retrieval System (MEDLARS), in terms of user services. ERIC is based on a number of clearinghouse in universities and other institutions across the country, plus a center in Washington, D.C., which process some 35,000 separate reports and another 20,000 articles published in periodicals. These materials are culled, abstracted, and indexed, and about a third of them are retained for dissemination across the nation. Users may read copyrighted articles and papers on microfiche provided to major libraires across the nation by ERIC, or they may obtain microfiche or hard copies at a nominal cost directly from the ERIC system.

Publishers were aware of ERIC's implications from the beginning. One observer chided in 1967 that, while ERIC had "doubtless laudable aims," it nonetheless had been seeking "blanket permissions to microfilm quantities of educational titles that are commercially published" and, furthermore, the "magic words 'education,' 'research,' and 'microfilm' are no substitute for sales . . . "

In this same year, an effort was made to resolve this conflict of interests between the U.S. Office of Education (USOE), and publishers. The American Book Publishers Council and the American Textbook Publishers Institute (ATPI) cooperated with USOE to form the Copyright Permissions Clearinghouse for Project ERIC. The ATPI managed the Clearinghouse for the benefit of the publishing industry. Each of the ERIC units responsible for indexing, abstracting, and reproducing articles for the system corresponded with the Copyright Permissions Clearinghouse in order to avoid infringement suits so that home and office terminals might be developed on a ground-up basis. EDUCOM's Task Force on Legal and Related Matters has been most effective in coming to grips with these difficulties.

Information systems that are organized around academic disciplines are particularly illustrative of the "political and sociological implications" of the electronic exchange of knowledge noted by EDUCOM. The National Science Foundation's Information System Program has been instrumental in forming the Chemical Abstracts Service System (CAS) of the American Chemical Society, the National Information System for Physics of the American Institute of Physics (both currently operative), the National Information System for Psychology (NISP) of the American Psychological Association, or APA (just beginning operations), and systems in linguistics and the life sciences (in planning stages). Of these, NISP and the information systems in chemistry are the most interesting if for entirely different reasons.

The National Information System for Psychology is of note because it dramatizes what information systems using neopublishing technologies can signify for the scholarly "establishments" in all disciplines. Like the systems in other fields, NISP has bibliographic retrieval, a system for exchanging informal communications, and a system for distributing tape cassettes and films. But it is unique in that it also has an early dissemination plan that would bypass journal editors and other more cumbersome academic referees altogether. Subscribers to NISP's early warning system would receive lists of unedited manuscripts and photocopies of those manuscripts in areas of their interests.

Early dissemination of unedited research has been questioned on intellectual grounds; some have objected that it will become "a vast sewer carrying garbage from one scientist to another." More significantly, perhaps, the circulating of manuscripts untouched, unread, and unevaluated by the academic establishment in psychology (especially the journal editors, who would seem most threatened by such a system), should intensify the apparently growing split between the pure research elite and the applied research mass of psychologists. Psychology journals are aimed primarily at researchers, while most APA members are engaged in nonresearch activities, such as clinical practice, teaching, or administration. Research psychologists comprise about fourteen percent of the APA's total membership of 30,000, and it is this segment that objects to the preprint publication scheme of NISP as unprofessional. One researcher complains that the "engineers and technicians have moved in and are pushing aside the psychologists . . . They want to do their thing rather than our thing. It's upside down." The researcher goes on to state that "control will slip away from research workers for whom the journals now exist as a medium." For what appears to be a majority of APA members, this may not be a bad turn of events.

It should be noted that elitist politics does not fully explain the intensity of the controversy in the American Psychological Association. Much of it is due to what is perceived as a "'cabal' . . . operating in relative secrecy . . . rushing pell-mell into a radical change . . . " But it is nevertheless noteworthy that an elite perceives its position to be threatened by the effective undercutting of its control of information and, concomitantly, status rewards.

The information systems in chemistry are interesting for reasons somewhat different than those of NISP. While the organization of the chemistry systems is diffused and complex, it is of such an order of comprehensiveness and sophistication that it appears to verge on attaining the total bibliographic automation of information.

The advanced stages of chemical information systems, in comparison to those of other disciplines, seem to be due to a greater receptivity to new information forms on the part of chemists, and to a longer history of information services. Chemical Abstracts has been an invaluable research tool of chemists for many years, and as early as 1946 the National Agricultural Library initiated a program of providing photographic copies of all articles listed in the Abstracts on request. The abstracts themselves are of such a high quality that the Service "rightly prides itself in stating that frequently it is unnecessary to read the original work . . . "

In the mid-1960s, the American Chemical Society was given funds by three federal agencies, in order that CAS could develop a Chemical Information System. The System is now operative, and data recorded on computer tapes can be retrieved by use of the article's title, journal citation, and author's name. Information abstracted from at least 600 primary journals is included, and abstracts from more than 11,000 additional journals related to chemistry are occasionally included.

Additional information access systems in chemistry are provided by the Institute for Scientific Information (ISI), a private organization based in Philadelphia. The Institute for Scientific Information publishes the Science Citation Index which, in the first six years of it's operation, cited some 4 million items, and Current Contents, an abstract service not only for chemistry, but for the life sciences, physics, education, engineering and technology, behavioral, social, and management sciences, and the agricultural, food, and veterinary sciences as well.

Index Chemicus, first published in 1960, since has been expanded to Current Abstracts of Chemistry and Index Chemicus, and surveys approximately 50,000 articles annually. In 1968, a computerized Index Chemicus Registry System was introduced, the first one ever to be commercially available and that provides data both in printed and tape formats.

The Institute for Scientific Information has approached the copyright problem via its Original Article Tear Sheet Service (OATS). The Institute buys multiple copies of journals, and the pages of articles literally are torn out for patrons. Only five or six issues of each journal are needed to supply OATS under normal circumstances. Photocopies also are furnished, but ISI has signed copyright agreements with leading publishers and pays royalties both for tear sheets and photocopies. The Institute for Scientific Information "takes great pride in the good relations it has maintained with publishers," and contends that the "growth in popularity of ISI's services has been paralleled by a comparable increase in journal circulation throughout the world."

Chemists do not think that the services provided by CAS, the American Chemical Society, and ISI are adequate. One chemist states that while CAS, for example, "supplies a workable research program . . . considerably improvement in speed and efficiency for large-scale processing is possible through reprogramming." To this end, chemical information centers have appeared within the last three years at the Universities of Pittsburhg, Georgia, and Louisville, the Illinois Institute of Technology Research Institute in the United States, and at the University of Nottingham in England. Most offer inexpensive data services based on Chemical Abstracts, and at least one is financed by the National Science Foundation. Pittsburgh's system provides bibliographic access via the author's name, key words in the title, author's country or place of work, coden designation of the journal, and citation. It also is possible to make a search in which structures or even substructures of compounds are used as search terms. The emergence of these centers suggests that, in the immediate future, computer-based search services will be supplied to chemists from a few regional dissemination centers, which will cooperate in the development of a national, and possibly of an international, network.

Perhaps more than other current information storage and retrieval systems, the developments in chemistry draw the greatest concern of copyright owners. One publisher has stated that the Chemical Information System could "give the Chemical Abstracts Service a virtual monopoly of basic chemical information . . . which will replace similar works in chemistry and chemical engineering that are now produced by commercial publishers. In effect, this Government activity may put an entire discipline of scientific information into the hands of a non-profit publishing monopoly."

MEDLARS and ERIC differ from the other systems discussed previously in that they not only are funded, but are operated by federal agencies. Founded in 1964, MEDLARS is directed by the National Library of Medicine (NLM). It stores, on magnetic tapes, citations to much of the world's biomedical literature and retrieves information electronically, making individual demand searches, producing bibliographies, and printing the Index Medicus by means of a computer. The MEDLARS system will encompass a Center for Biomedical Communications that will act as a central clearinghouse of health-related data, regional medical literature, local university and hospital libraries, and specialized information centers that would serve sunject areas on a national basis.

The MEDLARS service of providing hard copies of articles to physicians, researchers, and students on demand is of greatest pertinence to publishers. Although NLM officials expected regional and local libraries to handle ninety percent of the users' requests, more than 160,000 photocopied articles now are sent to users by MEDLARS each year.

To provide such a service as MEDLARS, the National Library of Medicine has had to develop one of the most highly sophisticated photocopying systems in any library today. The National Library of Medicine has developed a unique mobile camera; the camera van and operator go to the bound volumes on the shelves, rather than books being carried to the camera. Through the use of specially designed duplicating equipment, the microfilms are reproduced in finished copy for mailing to the requester.

Roger H. Smith, in an editorial in Publishers' Weekly, praised the clearinghouse idea as a "creative, if modest, search for an answer" in relating copyrights to computers. He went on to express his "hope that publishers, in setting their permission policies, will be sufficiently flexible to give the Clearinghouse a chance to work. The permissions granted to ERIC, after all, will be of short duration: two years after which ERIC's computers will erase all the material they have received under the project."

In 1969, the same magazine announced the discontinuance of ERIC's Copyright Permissions Clearinghouse, and notified its readers that individual units "in the ERIC system will now correspond directly with permissions departments of those publishers from which they desire permission for microfiche or hard copy reproduction."

Systems such as NISP, CAS, MEDLARS, ERIC, and others represent sizable accomplishments in large-scale information storage and retrieval systems. But ever larger systems loom in the future. The Committee on Scientific and Technical Information, EDUCOM, the Committee on National Library Information Systems (a group of library and documentation associations), and the President's National Advisory Commission on Libraries all have proposed variants of national networks in which libraries would be "nodes" connected by "links" of transmission lines of various kinds. But of ultimately greater significance is the proposal for a worldwide science information system, a proposal four years in the making.

The title of the proposed system is UNISIST (United Nations Information System in Science and Technology) and is the product of a joint effort by the United Nations Educational, Scientific, and Cultural Organization and the International Council of Scientific Unions. Its ultimate goal is the establishment of a network of information services based on voluntary cooperation, and much of the suggested UNISIST structure would be based on existing systems centered in national governments and professional societies.

Proponents of UNISIST are aware that in the past such schemes for "a gigantic organization" were "doomed to failure" for "technical, financial, and political reasons." But today evidence exists that indicates these hindrances of the past are waning due to increasing cooperation among libraries, to burgeoning volumes of scientific literature, to demands of scientists for a reassembling of information, and to governmental awareness that scientific and technical information is a national resource. Proponents of UNISIST argue that "no branch of science or national government can afford to pile incompatible data files on top of incompatible program languages on top of incompatible National systems to build a new tower of Babel. An international effort is of prime importance."

Publishers already have registered their objections to UNISIST on the ground that it smells of "anticopyright sentiment" and promotes "a worldwide doctrine of 'fair use' (i.e., 'free use') on sci-tech materials . . . giving developing countries almost carte blanche to republish . . . material first published in 'developed' countries." It is true that proponents of UNISIST tend to view copyright as an obstacle to the optimal dissemination of research, particularly in the less developed nations, but UNISIST's supporters hope to allay copyright owners' fears by keeping its activities mainly in the governmental sphere, where the public domain policy often applies to published works.

CABLE TELEVISION: THE LAST LINKAGE

In considering the development of new information technologies, we must introduce a technology that symbolizes the merging of information and communication capacities: CATV, an acronym that stands for cable television or community antenna television. CATV has had its own political history in the copyright dispute. It is more entertainment than educationally oriented (for the moment), is more iconic than symbolic as a medium than are the neopublishing technologies and, strictly speaking, is a communications technology rather than an information technology. For these reasons, CATV has not been central to this discussion. Nevertheless, when we confront the information utilities of the future and indulge in technological forecasting, cable television must be recognized as equal in importance to the neopublishing technologies.

CATV was born in the minds of frustrated citizens living in small towns. Residents of Lancaster, Pennsylvania, and Astoria, Oregon, decided during the years 1948, 1949, and 1950 to erect community antennae, link them via coaxial cables to their homes, and thus improve their television receptions. They did, and it worked. By 1952, there were seventy CATV systems with 20,000 subscribers in the United States.

CATV has immense potential as a communications technology. From its modest beginnings in Pennsylvania and Oregon, by 1972 there were an estimated 3,500 CATV systems operating in 15 percent of American homes with television, reaching 8,300,000 subscribers, generating $500 million worth of revenues for CATV operators annually, and producing $120 million worth of sales in CATV equipment each year. As a rough indicator, CATV should be in 50 percent of U.S. homes with television (98 percent of all American households have television) by 1975. This tremendous growth is attributable largely to the popularity of color television (30 percent of U.S. homes have color sets), and the availability of more programming channels. Both color reception and channel availability are facilitated in all topographies by CATV. Importantly, local cable systems can be economically viable on very small scales; the average American CATV system had less than 3,000 subscribers in 1973.

In terms of ability to transmit information to homes and businesses, the coaxial cables of CATV have considerably more potentiality than do telephone wires. CATV, particularly when integrated with the very new and developing microwave communications technology, which is designed specifically for data transmission, may provide the final link needed for massive information networks that serve the nation, home by home and office by office.

Precisely what form the home information terminal of the future might take is speculative, but it probably would combine the features of a television set, telephone, typewriter, and possibly photocopier, and would offer library, research, news, entertainment, and educational services. These utilities would be true networks, allowing participants to exchange information over geographic space very rapidly and on demand.

Edwin B. Parker and Donald A. Dunn, professors of communications and of engineering economic systems at Stanford University, estimate that the capital cost per subscriber of such a network would be from $500 to $700 excluding the expense of a television set. This is the rough equivalent of the capital investment for the current telephone plant in the United States, and would have approximately the same pervasiveness of service. Annual operating costs of the information utility also would parallel those of the present telephone system, which is about $130 per telephone. Parker and Dunn argue that most U.S. homes could have an information utility by 1985, if policy research, experimentation, and private development were encouraged adequately at the federal level. Early work by private firms, such as IBM, Microwave Communications, Inc., Mitre Corporation, and the quasi-private Rand Corporation, attests to the practicality of the information utility idea.

A SCENARIO

If cable television and microwave communications were fostered intellegently by public policy-makers, a logical next phase would be cooperation between CATV operators, microwave interests, and computer firms, in order that home and office terminals might be developed on a ground-up basis.

Time-sharing computing services also are a growing industry, and we may expect these firms to indulge in joint ventures with computer hardware companies and CATV interests. The continuing development of facsimile transmission technology, in which paper copies are transmitted over telephone wires, also would appear to offer the possibility of establishing highly reader-specialized news services in a vaguely traditional format. The Japanese daily _Asahi Shibun_ developed an inexpensive Telenews system by 1969 that printed newspapers in the home, and Matsushita Industries has a similar prototype called TV Fax.

A user could store information in a variety of formats. Paper and microform facsimiles, computer memory banks that use modified television sets as display terminals, and the infant technologies of casettes and electronic video recording devices are only some possibilities.

Research libraries would seem to be the most likely institutional locus for the initial development of national information networks. Already ERIC, MEDLARS, and even interlibrary loans of books and photocopied articles comprise library-based information systems that have the potentiality for evolving into national networks. More likely, however, intercampus experiments will constitute the first true information networks, i.e., systems that exchange data between several nodes over geographic space, rather than sending user requests to a central clearinghouse. Even so, Systems Data Corporation and Lockheed Corporation already are operating on-line networks, and these and other private companies may outstrip developments in education.

From the bounds of the campus, information technology should spill over into elementary and secondary schools. Teaching machines, as Anthony G. Oettinger, Director of Harvard University's Computing Center, has noted, comprise the foundation of a technological myth that is bought (all too literally) in its entirety by educational professionals. Oettinger is particularly critical of costly but delicate "junk" that is inappropriate for the penknife realities of the classroom. But recent work by D. Alpert and D. L. Bitzer on the Plato IV system at the University of Illinois appears to offer some reason for believing in the eventual development of practical, rugged, and effective teaching machinery.

In fact, the interfaces between elementary, secondary, and higher educational systems would appear to be a series of two-way technological streets. It seems likely that research-oriented information networks will attend downward from the apex of education's pyramidal structure and that the scope of computerized instructional devices will extend upwards from its base. Elementary school teachers are the teaching machine's fondest friends. R. Louis Bright, former U.S. Associate Commissioner of Education for Research, has predicted that the majority of American elementary schools will have computer-managed instruction by 1978, and that computerized teaching should spread to secondary schools and junior colleges in less than twenty years.

As the institutional base of information networks shifts from the university to the secondary and elementary school and homogenizes with the established technological foundation of computerized instructional devices, the financial base of information networks probably shift with it. The current money for information network development comes principally from federal agencies and private foundations. We can expect future financing to be on a more commercial footing involving corporations representative of the present membership of the Information Industry Association: educational publishers, photocopier and teaching machine manufacturers, and computer firms.

From the school house it is only a short distance to the home. Initial consumer-oriented experiments probably will involve networks concerned with games, household computations, and stock market and similar financial services, in short, toys for the rich. But by the time home information terminals are marketable, there should be some competition in the private sphere, and a variety of services will be available. The locus of business activity in this stage probably will be centered in the large computer, photocopier, microtechnology, television, telephone, and general electronics firms.

Finally, we might conceive an integrating of all information networks in the form of public information utilities. In such a utility, all the major information resources of the society would be interconnected and accessible via home-based terminals. Libraries, schools, governments, businesses, universities, news services, entertainment, in short, all organizations and institutions that produce data, would be linked to each citizen through an incredibly vast system of electronic information networks.

So much for our scenario. While it may not prove accurate, it is at least reasonable given present circumstances. When we recall the novelty of the telephone in 1900, of radio in 1920, of television in 1950, and of the photocopier and computer in 1960, the scenario hypothesized here does not seem too "far out."

REFERENCES

Alpert, D. and Bitzer, D. L. (1970). Advances in computer-based education. Science CLXVII, March 20, 1582-1590.

Beer, Stafford (1970). "Managing Modern Complexity." The management of information and knowledge. A compilation of papers prepared for the Eleventh Meeting of the Panel on Science and Technology, Committee on Science and Astronautics, U.S. House of Representatives. Washington: U.S. Government Printing Office, 41-62.

Bengelsdorf, Irving S. (1970). The information utility and social change. In The information utility and social choice, Harold Sackman and Norman Nie (Eds.). Montvale, New Jersey: AFIPS Press, 167-181.

Benjamin, Curtis G. (1966). Copyright and government. Library Journal XCI, February 15, 881-886.

Boffey, Philip M. (1970). Psychology: Apprehension over a new communications system. Science CLXVII, February 27, 1228-1230.

Breedin, Brent (1970). Informal tour of the national center for higher education. College & Uiversity Journal IX, Winter, 17-32.

Brown, George W., Miller, James G., and Keenan, Thomas A., (Eds.) (1967), EDUNET. Report of the Summer Study on Information Networks conducted by the Interuniversity Communications Council (EDUCOM). New York: John Wiley and Sons, Inc.

Brown, Ralph S., Jr. (1969). Appendix: Copyright problems of research libraries. In On Research Libraries. Statement and recommendations of the Committee on Research Libraries of the American Council of Learned Societies. Submitted to the National Advisory Commission on Research Libraries, November, 1967. Cambridge, Massachusetts: The M.I.T. Press, 86-100.

Brudner, Harvey J. (1968). Computer-managed instruction. Science 162, November 29, 970-976.

Burke, John Emmett (1966). The rising tide — more research libraries. Commerce, Texas: East Texas State University.

Busha, Charles H. and Landrum, John H. (1967). "Telefacsimile communication with the Xerox Magnavox Telecopier in reference to interlibrary loans: A report of a three-month experimental demonstration conducted by the South Carolina State Library Board." Columbia, South Carolina: South Carolina State Library Board, July.

Clapp, Verner W. (1968). The copyright dilemma: A librarian's view. Library Quarterly XXXVIII, October, 352-387.

Davis, Watson (1967). The universal brain: Is centralized storage and retrieval of all knowledge possible, feasible, or desirable? In The growth of knowledge: Readings on organization and retrieval of information, Manfred Kochen (Ed.). New York: John Wiley and Sons, Inc., 60-65.

Denison, E. F. (1962). "Sources of economic growth in the United States and the alternatives before us." New York: Committee for Economic Development.

de Solla Price, Derek J. (1967). Networks of scientific papers. In *The growth of knowledge: Readings on organization and retrieval of information*, Manfred Kochen (Ed.). New York: John Wiley and Sons, Inc., 145-155.

Dunlop, Robert A. (1970). The emerging technology of information utilities. In *The information utility and social choice*, Harold Sackaman and Norman Nie (Eds.). Montvale, New Jersey: AFIPS Press, 25-50.

Federal Council for Science and Technology, Committee on Scientific and Technical Information, Ad Hoc Task Group on Legal Aspects Involved in National Information Systems (1967). *The Copyright Law as It Relates to National Information Programs*. A Study by the ad hoc Task Group on Legal Aspects Involved in National Information Systems, PB-175 168, July, 1967. Washington: U.S. Government Printing Office, p. 81.

Garfield, Eugene (1964). Abstracting and Problems of Copyright. In *Reprography and copyright law*, Lowell H. Hattery and George P. Bush (Eds.). Baltimore, Maryland: Port City Press, Inc., 112-118.

A giant rival for the top copier cat (1970). *Business Week* *No. 2121*, April 25, 33-34.

Gipe, George A. (1967). *Nearer to the dust: Copyright and the machine*. Baltimore: Williams and Wilkins Press, 1967.

Greenberger, Martin, Aronofsky, Julius, McKenney, James L., and Massy, William F. (1973). Computer and information networks. *Science* *182*, October 5, 29-35.

(1964). Reprographic technology: Present and future. In *Reprography and copyright law*, Lowell H. Hattery and George P. Bush (Eds.). Baltimore, Maryland: Port City Press, Inc., 139-147.

Hawken, William R. (1964). Reprographic technology: Present and future. In *Reprography and copyright law*, Lowell H. Hattery and George P. Bush (Eds.). Baltimore, Maryland: Port City Press, Inc., 39-49.

Holden, Constance (1970). APA information plan funded. *Science* *CLXX*, December 25, 1385.

Institute for Scientific Information. *The who and why of ISI* (pamphlet). Philadelphia: Institute for Scientific Information (undated, unnumbered).

Kestenbaum, Lionel (1970). The Regulatory Context of Information Utilities: Varieties in Law and Public Policy. In The information utility and social choice, Harold Sackman and Norman Nie (Eds.). Montvale, New Jersey: AFIPS Press, 73-101.

Kleinschrod, W. A. (1963). Unscrambling the claims about copies: AM looks at 174 machines and processes new and old. Administrative Management XXIV, March, 42-64.

Koepke, John C. (1964). Assessment of documentation practices in reprography. Reprography and copyright law, Lowell H. Hattery and George P. Bush (Eds.). Baltimore, Maryland: Port City Press, Inc., 50-58.

Loevinger, Jane (1970). Letters. Science CLXVIII, April 10, 194.

A Look at Where EDUCOM Now Stands and the Goals It Hopes to Accomplish (1967). EDUCOM: Bulletin of the Interuniversity Communications Council II, January, 2-3.

Massy, William F. (1974). Computer networks: Making the decision to join one. Science 186, November 1, 414-420.

Mathews, Max V. and Brown, W. Stanley (1969). Research Libraries and the New Technology. On research libraries. Statement and recommendations of the Committee on Research Libraries of the American Council of Learned Societies. Submitted to the National Advisory Commission on Research Libraries, November, 1967. Cambridge, Massachusetts: The M.I.T. Press, 59-76.

Mohrhardt, Foster E. (1964). Government library, documentation and information interests in copyright. In Reprography and copyright law, Lowell H. Hattery and George P. Bush (Eds.). Baltimore, Maryland: Port City Press, Inc., 99-104.

Monk, Peter K. (1970). The national library of medicine. In The Bowker annual of library and book trade information, 1970, Carole Collins and Frank L. Schick (Eds.). New York: R. R. Bowker, 251-257.

Federal Council for Science and Technology. Committee on Scientific and Technical Information. Ad Hoc Task Group on Legal Aspects Involved in

Moran, Leila P. (1970). The national agricultural library. In The Bowker annual of library and book trade information, 1970, Carole Collins and Frank L. Schick (Eds.). New York: R. R. Bowker, 247-250.

Morehouse, H. G. and Schoffner, R. M. (1966). An experiment in library application of Xerox LDX Facsimile Transmission Equipment. Phase I: Planning and Analysis. Sponsored by the Council on Library Resources, Inc., Washington, D.C., Report No. CLR-340. Berkeley, California: Institute of Library Research, University of California, June 13.

Nelson Associates, Inc. (1968). "An Evaluation of the New York State's Pilot Program in the Facsimile Transmission of Library Materials." Sponsored by the Division of Library Development, New York State Library, Albany, New York. Thornwood, New York: Commerce Offset, February.

Nelson Associates, Inc. (1968). "The New York State Library's Pilot Program in the Facsimile Transmission of Library Materials: A Summary Report." Thornwood, New York: Commerce Offset, June.

Oettinger, Anthony G. with Marks, Sema (1969). Run, computer, run: The mythology of educational innovation. Cambridge, Massachusetts: Harvard University Press.

Platt, John Rader (1966). The step to man. New York: John Wiley and Sons.

Rx for MDs: Citation by automation (1966). EDUCOM: Bulletin of the Interuniversity Communications Council I, September, 4-8.

Smith, Roger H. (1967). An effort to relate copyrights & computers. Publishers' Weekly CXCII, September 4, 38.

Teplitz, Arthur (1970). Microfilm and Reprography. In Annual review of information science and technology: Volume 5, 1970, Carols A. Cuadra and Ann W. Luke (Eds.). American Society for Information Science. Chicago: William Benton, Publisher, 87-111.

Tocatlian, Jacques J. (1971). A world science information system. Scholarly Publishing II, January, 203-207.

Two gee-whiz giants go at each other (1970). Business Week No. 2128, June 13, 70-82.

Warthman, Forrest (1974). Telecommunication and the City. The Annals of the American Academy of Political and Social Science. "The Information Revolution," Donald M. Lamberton (Special Ed.) 412, March, 127-137.

Williams, Edwin E. (1969). "Bibliographical Control and Physical Dissemination," On Research Libraries. Statement and recommendations of the Committee on Research Libraries of the American Council of Learned Societies. Submitted to the National Advisory Commission on Research Libraries, November, 1967. Cambridge, Massachusetts: The M.I.T. Press, 26-58.

Woodward, F. Peter (1967). Sounder thinking through clearer writing. Science CLVI, May 12, 743-745.

Xerox's new anti-IBM machine (1970). Business Week No. 2125, May 23, 42-44.

Zeidler, H. M., Lipinsky, A. J., Moll, L. J., Shapiro, E. B., Kent, W. A., and Wensley, J. H. "Patterns of Technology and Data Communications." Report No. 7379B-4. Stanford, California: Stanford Research Institute, N.D.

Chapter 3

SOCIETY, TECHNOLOGY, AND COPYRIGHT

As we noted in the preceding chapter, the data technology explosion is comparable in its magnitude and exponentiality to the data explosion itself. The effects of the new information technologies on traditional public policies for public knowledge, notably copyright law, are profound, and this chapter and the next suggest that copyright no longer may be suitable as a policy for the creation and dissemination of information in technological societies such as ours.

THE DEVELOPMENT OF U.S. COPYRIGHT LAW AS A RESPONSE TO TECHNOLOGY

In the West, copyright is distinctly related to the acceptance of John Locke's philosophy that a primary function of government is the protection of property, and to the exceptional profitability of publishing at the beginning of the eighteenth century. The first copyright law appeared in Queen Anne's England in 1710, and it marked the initiation of a Western mind-set that continues to interrelate protectionism, printing, and intellect.

The law and logic of copyright protection were firmly established in the minds of early American political thinkers before the Republic was founded. Individual petitioners were applying to state legislators for the exclusive right to copy and vend their printed works before the Revolutionary War had run its course. The first granting of such a right was to one Andrew Law, in 1779, by the Connecticut Assembly. Law had compiled, engraved, and printed a _Collection of the Best Tunes for the Promotion of Psalmody_, and argued that "works of Art ought to be protected in this Country," at least for five years duration.

In 1783, John Ledyard made a similar plea to the Connecticut Assembly. The legislators, in granting his petition for the protection of the Journal of Captain Cook's Last Voyage to the Pacific Ocean, also passed the first American copyright act. In the same year Massachusetts, Maryland, New Jersey, New Hampshire, and Rhode Island also enacted copyright statutes. Virginia adopted copyright in 1785, and New York in 1786. Of the original colonies, only Delaware failed to establish a copyright law. Much of this activity stemmed from the efforts of individual petitioners. Of special note are the efforts of Noah Webster to secure protection for his grammar book, the memorial before Congress in 1782 of Connecticut's Joel Barlow, which urged that the states consider the passage of copyright laws, and James Madison's report to the Continental Congress of 1783, which favored copyright legislation of fourteen years duration.

Madison, father of the Constitution and ever the intellectual, also promoted a national copyright act in The Federalist Papers. In No. 43 he wrote that the "utility of this power will scarcely be questioned," indicating the almost apolitical character that the English copyright concept already had assumed. Madison added that the "copyright of authors has been solemnly adjudged in Great Britain to be a right of common law . . . The public good fully coincides with the claims of individuals."

It is not surprising that Article 1, Section 8, of Madison's Constitution of 1787 states that Congress shall have the power "to promote the Progress of Science and Useful Arts, by securing for limited times to Authors and Inventors the exclusive Right to their respective Writings and their Discoveries." Nor is it surprising that Congress passed the first Copyright Act in 1790.

Since then United States copyright law has been revised three times: in 1831, in 1870, and in 1909. Copyright laws in this country have stood unrevised for periods of roughly forty years, with the exceptions of the current act, which has survived intact for more than sixty-five years.

Perhaps the most notable trend in these revisions is that the period of copyright duration has increased steadily. Copyright protection has been extended from two years, to fourteen, to twenty-one, to twenty-eight, to its present fifty-six. The current revision bill would extend this period to the author's lifetime plus fifty years, a duration amounting to approximately seventy-six years on the average (or eighty-six years according to other calculations).

The last revision, in 1909, began at least eight years earlier, when the first Register of Copyrights, Thorvald Solberg, suggested the need for revision in each of his annual reports from 1901 through 1904. President Theodore Roosevelt called for a new copyright law in December 1905. The process of revising the law between 1905 and 1909 had some striking similarities to the current revision effort. The Copyright Office (which had been established only in 1897) served as a secretariat to the appropriate House and Senate committees and drafted and redrafted bills. Hearings included representative organizations of librarians, authors, educational institutions, dramatists, bar associations, advertising agencies, photoengravers, photographers, theater managers, composers, architects, and a variety of publishers. Private conferences were held between all these peak associations, legislators, and Copyright Office officials. The major controversies surrounding the 1909 Act were the use of copyrighted music on mechanical instruments (e.g., piano rolls and records), and public libraries purchasing books printed abroad. Roosevelt, a man long interested in science and literature, summoned the antagonists to a White House meeting and forcefully helped the factions iron out their differences.

The 1909 Act had been a response to "modern conditions," as President Roosevelt called them. Roosevelt had drawn attention to the fact that American "copyright laws urgently need revision . . . they omit provision for many articles which, under modern reproductive processes, are entitled to protection." Notably, the new law of 1909 did not meet copyright owners' demands in this respect. An editorial in Publishers' Weekly stated that the Act had made "an important stride in American copyright, though it falls far short of the aims and hopes of the friends of copyright." One wonders what, precisely, the friends of copyright had in mind. The Act defined copyright (as it still does) as the "exclusive right" of the copyright proprietor "to print, reprint, publish, copy, and vend the copyrighted work." Such a definition is, to put it mildly, a no-nonsense statement.

Between 1909 and 1924, six revision bills were introduced in order that the United States might enact a copyright law that adhered to the International Copyright Convention, usually referred to as the Berne Convention. No action was taken on any of the bills. From 1926 to 1941, five individual amendments were passed that altered minor portions of the 1909 law. In 1948, the United Nations Educational, Scientific, and Cultural Organization initiated a series of meetings that developed the Universal Copyright Convention, which was signed in 1952 by forty countries, including the United States, at Geneva. The Senate Foreign Relations and Judiciary Committees held joint hearings on the Geneva Convention, and on the relatively minor amendments to U.S. copyright law that were required by the Convention. Ratification of the Convention and the amendments were passed in 1954.

In 1955, Congress commissioned the U.S. Copyright Office to initiate studies on the possibility of a revised copyright law. These thirty-four scholarly articles marked both an end and a beginning. The end to any possibility for a privately negotiated agreement between copyright owners and users over the roles of new information technologies in copyright arrangements was signalled by the decision to alter national law. The beginning of a long, occasionally vituperative, occasionally statesmanlike political controversy was heralded by the same decision. It continues today.

IDEAS AS PROPERTY

While copyright as a public policy for the origination and dissemination of knowledge has undergone many modifications since 1710, its fundamental assumption about the nature of knowledge has remained unaltered. To wit: Ideas are property, specifically intellectual property, and therefore must be managed according to proprietary concepts. The assumption that copyrighted information is private intellectual property and thus, like land, subject to the perquisites of its owner, is an important one. On it rests the legal sanctions of the state that prohibit the unauthorized copying of information protected by copyright, thereby restricting the completely free use of knowledge. Neopublishing technologies not only have undercut owners' control of information, but in the process have reduced the potency of the state to enforce its own laws. By implication, these technologies have called into question the ability of the state generally to protect the property of its citizens.

But can information every really be "property"? And, if it is, should it be?

The notion that copyright sanctions a property right is supported by copyright owners. The reasoning here is that the author owns his writing because he wrote it, much like General Motors Corporation owns a Chevrolet prior to sale because it made the car. In the same vein, the publisher owns the copyrighted work because (1) the author gave him his permission to sell his creation, (2) the publisher also has made a product by converting a manuscript into a format fit for sale, and (3) has invested and risked his capital in doing so.

Values symbolized by the knee-jerk phrases of private property, capitalism, laissez faire, and free enterprise are associated with this construct. A spokesman for copyright owners has argued before Congress that, "If we are to retain a private sector in our economy, if we are not to have a nationalized utility or a nationalized industry, either a Government sponsored or supervised information and knowledge utility, we must retain the private competitive sector." Copyright is seen not only as the optimal means of creating and distributing data, but of preserving the values represented by free enterprise as well.

Copyright users have not had the temerity to deny flatly that copyright protects property. Rather, they say that copyright protects a nasty kind of property: monopoly. Users trot out their own catchwords, such as academic freedom, research, service, and education, and then relate the values they encompass to evils long associated with "cornering the market." The benefits symbolized by education can never be fully realized so long as profiteers control the knowledge market. A representative of copyright users has testified in hearings that, "Even at its best . . . a copyright necessarily involves the right to restrict as well as to monopolize the diffusion of knowledge," and that this unseemly power is in conflict with "the paramount public interest in the United States . . . its system of public and private schools which reaches into every home into every corner of the Nation."

Whether or not copyright protects "information monopolies" or sanctifies private "intellectual property," the point stands that both copyright owners and users have accepted and are rooted in a traditional conventional widsom, that knowledge is somehow "property." This is a questionable premise.

Property, as it normally is understood, is something tangible, substantial and, as such, measurable and divisible, land, for instance. When these criteria are applied to thoughts, however, they seem grotesquely ill-suited. Do the precious, abstracted distinctions that an English teacher makes between words and phrases in a poem by T. S. Eliot strike us as tangible? Substantial? Can his distinctions be measured and divided into quantifiable parts, as land can be? Can any idea be so parceled? No. At best an idea can be parsed, but only when it is in the format of a sentence. And what about ideas in other formats, such as painting or sculpture? Can we divide works in those formats and still retain their respective ideas? Not many people would be willing to buy a piece of canvas cut from Picasso's <u>Guernica</u>, no more than half an idea drawn from Joyce's <u>Portrait</u>. A parcel of land, however, even part of a car, is quite another matter.

Even when we rely on the more technical conceptualizations of property developed by economists, we find that the concept of intellectual property is unsatisfactory. By <u>private property</u>, economists mean goods that a person may dispose of as he sees fit. While books and essays may be disposed of in this manner, ideas cannot. Can we believe, for instance, that American policymakers saw fit to dispose of the idea of a hydrogen bomb to the Russians in the early 1950s.

Public property, on the other hand, belongs to the government, and the government may dispose of it. The notion that certain ideas belong to the government, and thus may be harbored or distributed by it, would seem to warrant an abrupt termination of this line of reasoning for reasons of censorship.

Finally, common property refers to goods that belong to all, and thus are controlled by no one. This would appear to be a more fruitful approach, except that it disallows remuneration to those who create ideas. Common property, because it is open to all, ultimately is consumed by all. For example, the oceans and air are common properties that soon may be consumed (i.e., effectively destroyed) by those who use them as bins for their pollutants. To treat ideas as common property by never paying for their production in forms capable of dissemination, conceivably could result in the partial destruction of idea-origination.

Ideas, it would appear, are not property. They are ideas. At best, ideas are products which can be owned only when rendered into those particular formats that are protected by copyright laws.

Given this, the question still to be addressed is: Why has the notion that ideas constitute property endured for more than 250 years? One reason for this endurance is the presence of certain moral justifications that intellectual creations ought to be owned by their creators. The fruits-of-their-labor argument is one of these, i.e., authors should be rewarded for the fruits of their labor. But this contention does not demonstrate that the sum a writer receives under present copyright arrangements is any more just than it would be under a different system of compensation.

A second ethical justification is that society ought to reward the authors of great works. Copyright, of course, does not do this. Instead, it rewards popularity, and the writer of lasting art is compensated only when he is fortunate enough to be appreciated by (or sold to) the Great Unwashed, as well as by his fellow artists. Herman Wouk's observation that Wolfe and Joyce were living from hand to mouth on small royalty checks at the height of their popularity is hardly a reason to maintain the status quo.

More pointedly, the belief that intellectual creations are property has survived as an operating premise of the law because it has been extrememly efficient economically. When printing was the only information technology of any significance, eighteenth-century policymakers conceived of an arrangement for knowledge-dissemination and compensation in society that was elegant in its absence of centralization and administration. Lawyers set up the machinery by granting exclusive rights to copy to those who wrote and to those who controlled presses; Adam Smith's "invisible hand" took care of the details. As Madison noted, copyright provided an efficient means of achieving the constitutional goal of promoting science and useful arts because it was one of those fortuitous policies in which the ends of the individual citizen and the goals of the collectivity could be made synonymous. Copyright, in short, was not a bad idea at the time.

Today, however, all of us can print, and print cheaply. Presses, as a means of production, no longer are controlled only by those who have invested their capital in them. Everyone has access to some form of publishing instrument. As a result, the continuance of copyright on the proprietary logic that it is the most efficient public policy for information creation and distribution no longer seems valid.

COPYRIGHT AND MARKET POWER: THE CASE OF BOOK PUBLISHING

An aspect of the proprietary premise of copyright as a public policy is that of economic power in the knowledge market. While the accusations of monopoly voiced by copyright users may sound shrill, they nonetheless are accusations that warrant some dispassionate analysis.

Upon examination, it turns out that there are reasons for believing that some facets of copyright have encouraged monopolistic tendencies in the knowledge market. This is particularly true for the book publishing industry. The 1972 Industry Statistics published by the Association of American Publishers states that 1972 pretax profits of adult hardbound tradebook publishers as a percentage of sales was 7.0 percent, 7.4 percent for science, social science, and technology book publishers, 9.1 percent for juvenile tradebook publishers, 12.5 percent for mass-market paperback publishers (nine such publishers responding) and also for "elhi" (for elementary and high school textbook publishers, twenty-four responding), 12.8 percent for medical book publishers, a 13.2 percent profit was reaped by the sundry book clubs, and college textbook publishers topped the list with 13.4 percent in profits (thirty-two such publishers responding). Moreover, book sales are comparatively sluggish during the 1970s in comparison to the 1960s, when college textbook publishers, for example, raked in 19.7 percent in 1968 pretax profits, and sales rates often jumped at a rate of 9 percent a year.

Still, total receipts by American book publishers in 1972 was a record-breaking $3,177,200,000 despite declining sales in a few areas.

Books designed to convey ideas dominate the marketplace. In 1972, the books published by academic presses, professional books (e.g., law, medicine, business, social science, science, and technology), elhi texts, and college texts accounted for 41 percent of all book sales in 1972. By comparison, the combined sales of adult and juvenile tradebooks (both hardbound and paperbound) and mass market paperbacks comprised only 30 percent of all domestic sales in 1972. As an article in Publishers' Weekly concluded, the "book industry's stake in education is enormous," for the area accounted for a whopping 67 percent of total sales in this country in 1972. A total of 51 percent of all books sold in the United States during that year were channelled through schools and similar institutions (23 percent), college stores (17 percent), and libraries (11 percent).

College textbook publishers consistently reap the highest profits of any category of book publishers, and there is reason to believe that free competition is limited in this area, an area vital to the transmission of sophisticated thinking in virtually every field of human endeavor. Stephen Breyer, a Harvard law professor, has analyzed the profits of college textbook publishers and concluded that the average profits skimmed from college texts are at least 50 percent greater than the average profits in manufacturing. He attributes these extraordinarily fat profits in part to teachers who are "fairly insensitive to price" as they do not buy texts themselves.

Moreover, the Hunt Survey of 1968 indicated that the twelve largest publishers of college textbooks (each with annual sales in excess of $6 million), accounted for 81 percent of all college text sales reported. The Census Burea stated in 1963 that the eight largest textbook publishers (elhi and college texts were not distinguished) accounted for 54 percent of all sales, and that the eight largest general book publishers printed 46 percent of the market's books.

Finally, all segments of book publishing are given a quantum of market power via copyright that is denied to other industries. While copyright does not restrict competition among different book titles, it does prevent free competition between copies of the same title and, more importantly, allows a house to accumulate exclusive licenses to publish. Such a power, for example, permits a publisher to build "stables" of prestigious authors. Status-laden stables of authors tend to attract novice writers with promising manuscripts which, in turn, inhibits the entrance of new publishers into the marketplace, since they are less likely to get first crack at reading the best new efforts.

When entry becomes difficult (and the high profits of college text publishers indicate that an entry barrier may indeed exist for publishers in this field), established publishers find it easier to resist demands for higher royalties from their writing stables, and also to raise prices on their books. Restricting royalties and raising prices can limit both the numbers of titles produced and the books circulated.

THE ECONOMICS OF PHOTOCOPYING

If there are overtones of a monopolistic marketplace in the book publishing trade, such overtones reach a cacophonic level in the photocopying industry. In 1972, the Federal Trade Commission (FTC) brought suit against Xerox Corporation on the grounds that Xerox had monopolized the $1.7 billion office copier business. As we noted in the preceding chapter, Xerox's growth during the 1960s was indeed phenomenal. By 1972, however, the FTC charged that Xerox dominated the industry, controlling 60 percent of overall revenues in the entire office copier market, 86 percent of revenues generated by the rental of copying machines, and 95 percent of the submarket in plain paper machines.

While there may be a monopoly in the photocopier business, the effects of those same photocopiers have worked to undermine monopolistic tendencies in the publishing trade. This is because photocopiers tend to render copyright law unenforceable and, in effect, make everyone with access to a photocopier one's own publisher, thus reducing the control over the printing press as the major means of information production traditionally held by publishing houses.

When put in a national perspective, the extent of photocopying becomes awesome. In 1962, George Fry and Associates conducted a study of photocopying practices for the National Science Foundation, which usually is referred to as the Fry Report. John C. Koepke, its chief investigator, estimated that about 3,600,000,000 photocopies of copyrighted and uncopyrighted material were being produced annually. Gipe estimated that 10 billion photocopiers were made in 1965, and in that same year, the president of Xerox reported that "In 1961, roughly 9.5 billion copies were produced in this country, resulting in total income for the industry of about $500 million." In 1967, the Committee to Investigate Copyright Problems Affecting Communication in Science and Education (CICP), projected that more than 1.8 billion pages of the 3 billion pages that would be photocopied in 1969, would be copyrighted material. But in 1969, the vice-chairman of Xerox Corporation made the remarkable statement that "the United States produced 27.5 billion paper copies in 1967. And this figure just covers copiers and duplicators — it doesn't take into account the miles of copying spun from computers, or microfilm copies, or spirit and stencil machines."

If per-page photocopying costs continue their downward spiral (and there is scant reason to believe otherwise), these already impressive figures should expand. No doubt there is, as economic theorists insist, a point of diminishing returns. But where that point is, and when it will be reached, is quite unknown. Gipe notes that by 1965 it was possible to produce twenty-five or more single copies for $.005 per page. Irwin Karp, in the same year, stated that by using a relatively simple combination of a photocopier, a Colitho mat, and a multigraph machine, any user could make single copies for $0.008 per page. Fifty copies of a sixty-four page publication retailing for $3.75 could be reproduced by this technique for $.55 a copy.

The most solidly founded empirical study on the relation of copying costs to the popularity of photocopying is by the Arthur D. Little consulting firm. The firm concluded that photocopying technologies will improve in quality and versatility, that costs "can be expected to decline somewhat in the future," that great "continued growth must be anticipated, even if at a slightly lower rate, in both the number of machines installed and the number of copies produced," and that "there is broadening trend and incentive for the individual user to copy parts of books."

For a decade, a number of individuals and organizations have attempted to study empirically the patterns and economic effects of photocopying. The Freehafer Report of the Joint Libraries Committee on Fair Use in Photocopying (1961), which surveyed ten libraries, was the first such attempt. In 1962, the National Science Foundation commissioned George Fry and Associates to study the problem as it pertained to scientific and technical publications. This was a relatively more thorough survey that examined the effects of photocopying on authors, publishers, users, librarians, and manufacturers of copying machinery. In 1963, Robert F. Clarke, working under a grant from the U.S. Air Force, completed a doctoral dissertation in library science on the topic. He examined copying of dissertations by University Microfilms and photocopying of articles in science journals in a sample of major research libraries.

In 1966, the American Book Publishers Council (ABPC) and the American Textbook Publishers Institute (ATPI) sponsored the previously cited study by Arthur D. Little, Incorporated, to determine the impact of technology on publishing. The survey related decreasing photocopying costs to increasing photocopying use. In the same volume in which the Little study appeared, there was an empirical examination of copying practices in American education, conducted by the National Opinion

Research Center (NORC) at the request of the ABPC and the ATPI. The NORC study essentially was a combination of surveys, and indicated the widespread growth of photocopying practices in education.

The most prestigious of the surveys, perhaps, appeared the following year. The Committee to Investigate Copyright Problems was awarded a grant by the U.S. Office of Education to examine photocopying practices in libraries. Photocopies in sixty-six libraries were recorded for one month, and an extensive opinion questionaire sent to librarians. Former Register of Copyrights Abraham L. Kaminstein has said that the CICP is "probably the only organization that has tried to stay independent, or at least neutral, between the opposing sides," and is unique in that it "has tried to look at the situation and get the facts." The latest attempts to assess empirically photocopying practices are a two-week study of photocopying at the University of Toronto Library, and a twelve-month study of forty-one Canadian university libraries, which largely validate the CICP's findings.

These studies are both useful and useless. While they brought a number of empirical data to light, their conclusions are conflicting. Several of them are vague not only in terms of methodology, but of scope. Nor do their researchers seem to have precisely the same investigative missions. Most importantly, however, developing technology tends to data many of the studies' findings. Thus, one publisher, for example, has said that "As a consequence of rapid changes in technology, the cheerfully reassuring Fry Report of 1962 on photocopying is obsolete."

The studies' conclusions can be bisected crudely into two camps: pro-user and pro-owner. Pro-user conclusions are apparent or implied in the Freehafer Report (1961), the Fry Report (1962), the Blackburn study at the University of Toronto (1970), and the Stuart-Stubbs Canadian university study (1971). Pro-owner conclusions are apparent or implied in the Little Report (1966) and the NORC study (1966). The CICP Report (1967), while not definitive, does make an effort to avoid recommendations concerning a new copyright law, and tries to present only data. But the known sympathies of its authors for a copyright clearinghouse (discussed later in this chapter) seems to have made copyright users less favorable toward it than owners.

If the various studies point toward a single conclusion, it is that those owners most alarmed by photocopying are having their books copied least. The ratio of journal titles to books copied was nine to one, according to the CICP survey. The comparable Stuart-Stubbs study of Canadian libraries found that 34 percent of all materials copied were periodicals, and 27.2 percent were books. The great majority of all items copied was scientific or technical (41 to 100 percent). More than 80 percent of the material copied is less than five years old, according to the CICP. "The number of multiple copies of the same document made for the same client by U.S. libraries is almost negligible," according to the CICP, although the 1971 Canadian study found that 4 to 5 percent of Canadian publications were recopied. Nonprofit journal copying dominates profit journal copying almost two-to-one. For books, this ratio is one-to-two, relying again on CICP figures. About 5 percent of the publishers in the United States produce 40 percent of the material copied. Journal articles nearly always are copied whole, and books nearly always are copied in part. The "preponderance" of journals copied are American, according to the CICP survey, although Clarke found that "over fifty percent" of the journals copied were foreign, and that therefore "this could have no influence on American publishers." The CICP findings, however, represent a wider sample, and the 1971 Canadian study found that 47.2 percent (by far the highest) of all materials copied were American.

In summary, therefore, the most likely publisher to have a (single) copy made of his works is a sci-tech, nonprofit journal publisher in the United States, who has been in business only for the last five years. These are precisely the people who until recently have been the least concerned with the relationship of neopublishing technologies to copyright protection. Additionally, photocopying practices in libraries (i.e., single copies of articles and parts of books) seem to relate nearly with the proposed application of statutory fair use to library photocopying, as described in current copyright revision bills and House and Senate Reports. These two points are elaborated in later chapters.

The NORC survey provides more details, particularly in relation to copying practices in higher education as opposed to elementary and secondary education. Its coordinators, Philip Ennis and Federick A. Schlipf, found that copying of published material is considerably greater in colleges than in schools, which tend to photocopy administrative papers. When published works are copied in schools, textbooks are favored, followed by music scores, tests, and answer sheets. College personnel photocopy journals, monographs, and reference books, in that order of frequency.

Book publishers, largely because they, unlike journal publishers, are organized, have been able to object pulicly to several of the studies. Julius J. Marke notes that book publishers objected to the Fry Report on the grounds that it focussed on journals and libraries, rather than on books and schools. Since the appearance of the CICP, NORC, and Stuart-Stubbs reports, however, these arguments have been heard with less frequency.

Book publishers contend that, because of heavy initial costs, photocopying and other forms of neopublishing represent a serious threat to the origination of knowledge. A single high school textbook can require an investment of $50,000 while a series of elementary school textbooks will require as much as $1 million investment before it is ready for marketing. A new encyclopedia recently required $7 million in make-ready costs. Furthermore, it is argued, risks in the book publishing business are high. Publisher Lee C. Deighton contends that there "can be no way to know in advance that a book . . . will sell." While other industries can market test a product, publishers cannot until they have a full stock in warehouses, ready for sale.

Despite the facts that books are copied rarely when compared to journals, that tradebooks are seldom copied at all, and that approximately one-third of the portions of books that are copied are published by nonprofit organizations (according to the CICP survey), book publishers are prone to cite the Little Report, which projected a rise in book copying and a decrease in photocopying costs. Deighton stated in 1965 that "it is now possible to copy certain books at a cost less than the purchase price." That same year, the American Textbook Publishers Institute, in a letter to Senator John McClellan, Chairman of the Subcommittee on Patents, Trademarks, and Copyrights, submitted that 1964 per-page costs of textbook publishing were consistently higher than a photocopy of the same text: college texts had a per-page cost of $.008, high school texts cost $.006 per page to publish, elementary school texts were $.007 per page, and a photocopy of any text costs $.005 per page.

Nevertheless, the NORC study indicated that textbooks are still the mainstay in education. This is particularly true for elhi texts, "the average secondary school spends about $13,000 a year to buy textbooks and workbooks and about $100 a year to copy textbook and workbook pages."

In terms of college texts, a recent campus survey conducted by Gilbert Youth Research, Inc., for the College Division of the Association of American Publishers and the National Association of College Stores, indicated that photocopying cuts very little into textbook sales. Students estimated that they spent an average of $72 on books for the fall term of 1971, half of which was for assigned texts. Of those students who did not buy required books, 42 percent read the material in the college library, 41 percent borrowed a friend's copy, 12 percent went to the public library, and only 8 percent made a photocopy. The average university faculty member spent $115 in 1971 for professional books, and usually relied on library copies, reprints, and free desk copies from publishers to supplement his reading. If college textbook sales decline (and by 1972 this was beginning to happen), the study concluded, it probably will be attributable to the fact that about 60 percent of the faculty interviewed (68 percent of younger faculty members) foresee a decreasing importance of textbooks for teaching purposes.

Related to the college textbook market is the market for the scholarly monograph. Curtis G. Benjamin, former president of McGraw-Hill, has observed a steep decline in the sales of monographs, which he correlates with a rise in photocopying. The average sales of a single monograph over a period of five years since its initial publication sank from an average of 4,977 copies sold in 1957 to 2,961 copies in 1972. This reduced sales volume has served to raise the per-page cost of monographs by 144 percent over a fifteen year period (from 2.5 cents in 1957 to 6.1 cents in 1972). Benjamin argues that scholarly, particularly scientific, monographs must be protected from abuse by the new information technologies, notably photocopying. He predicts that, because of photocopying, "the scientific and technical monographs will disappear" as commercially viable publications by the end of the 1970s, and that the "other classes of scholarly books, including the bread-and-butter university press books, will lose their viability by the end of the 1980s."

While Benjamin's facts on monograph sales are undisputed, his reasoning that links their declining market to burgeoning photocopying practices is open to question. First, as Benjamin admits, he "cannot offer proof of the general point" that "uninhibited photocopying" is causing a sales slump in the scholarly book trade. Moreover, the fact stands that monographs still are profitable to publishers. Benjamin's company, McGraw-Hill, derives about 2 percent of its total operating profits from science and technology monographs, and, overall, such books accounted for approximately 7.4 percent of overall book publishing receipts in 1972. Secondly, empirical studies tend to deny that photocopying is a major underminer of monograph sales, if, indeed, it is at all. Vernon E. Palmour, principal investigator for a survey of interlibrary loan practices among eighty representative American academic libraries, found that of the probable 1,940,000 total loan requests in 1970, an estimated 668,000 such requests were for monographs. Of these, 21,400 requesters asked for photocopies of the monograph, and then only of limited portions of the publication. Hence, of the almost 2 million interlibrary loan requests in 1970, only 1 percent were requests for photocopies of sections of scholarly monographs! Moreover, only 71 percent of all loan requests actually were filled, and only 43 percent of those requests filled were supplied by photocopies. While interlibrary loan practices do not account for all photocopying in the country, the Palmour study would seem to indicate that relatively little photocopying is done of scholarly monographs.

Journal publishers appear to have considerably more reason for believing that photocopying may affect their profits, as their products are copied far more frequently. Koepke lists "three theoretical kinds of damage that the publisher of scientific and technical journals can sustain": damage to circulation, damage to advertising, and damage to reprint and back issue sales.

The reprint is, according to the Fry survey, still the medium of communication most preferred by scientists (73 percent of the Fry sample favored it), and photocopying has not substantially damaged reprint sales. Advertising losses resulting from photocopying are "the problem of the commercial publisher," whose periodicals are copied at a considerably less extensive rate than those of nonprofit journal publishers. The advertising argument holds that no advertiser will pay for advertising, because users will not photocopy advertisements. The Fry staff did not analyze empirically this facet in their survey, nor has anyone else.

The complaint that photocopying may diminish the circulation of some periodicals is one worthy of further examination. According to the Library of Congress, three new journals are born and one dies every day. Journal publishing, it may be presumed, is a highly marginal operation, and any financial loss due to inroads on journal circulation that is attributable to photocopying should be prevented if the unhindered dissemination of information is to be continued. This is particularly true of nonprofit journal publishers, who bear the brunt of photocopying practices.

Traditionally, and somewhat suprisingly, nonprofit journal publishers have not subscribed to this view. The Fry survey of 1962, which is the earliest investigation of the attitudes of periodical publishers, stated that the majority of journal publishers polled "encourage photoduplication of their journal articles" on the reasoning that the practice actually boosted the circulations of their publications via free advertising through the distribution of photocopied articles and acquainting librarians of their journals' existence by patrons requesting their journals' articles on interlibrary loan. This generalization, however, did not apply to "the giants of the industry," who associated (and continue to associate) photocopying with a loss in issue sales and subscription orders. In the mid-1960s a survey by the dean of the University of Maryland's School of Library and Information Services validated the Fry findings on the attitudes journal publishers, but by 1969 a study by Librarian Matt Roberts of 255 periodical publishers indicated a possible attitudinal shift. Although 72 percent of the respondents extended overall permission to a librarian's request to make five photocopies of single articles for reserve use, a majority of these attached "certain conditions" to their permission, and 16 percent flatly refused permission.

Currently, there are growing indications of rising concern and possible pro-owner sentiments among nonprofit journal publishers: The American Institute of Physics (whose seven member societies publish thirty-nine journals) and the American Chemical Society (representing twenty publications) filed amicus curiae briefs on the behalf of copyright owners in a recent court suit on photocopying and copyright; the American council of Learned Societies (with thirty-four member organizations) long has been pro-owner in its position (although a shift in position is occurring); and fourteen academic and publishing societies (several of which are pro-owner in their views) formed a Copyright Study Group that has sponsored a treatise, compiled by the Cambridge Research Institute, on the topic of copyright revision. Still, it would be premature to state categorically that the scholarly associations and nonprofit journal publishers are pro-owner; a number of library, dental, medical, and educational organizations have filed pro-user amicus curiae briefs in the above mentioned court case, including the Modern Language Association, the American Library Association, the National Education Association, the American Council on Education, and the History of Science Association, among others.

Part of this attitudinal ambiguity among nonprofit journal publishers on the role of photocopying and information dissemination stems from a cloudy correlation between the number of subscribers that a nonprofit journal has, and its potential for financial survival. A 1962 survey of 262 representatives scientific journals conducted by the National Science Foundation revealed that 211 were published by nonprofit scientific societies, 18 by university presses, and 33 by commercial publishing firms. The society journals, which comprised more than 80 percent of the sample, derived only 41 percent of their annual incomes from subscriptions. Journals published by university presses received 56 percent of their income from subscribers. No figure was given for the commercially published journals, although subscriptions account for 65 percent of this income drawn by the Williams and Williams Company's 30 journals, which are commercial publications. The major (and rising) source of income, certainly for nonprofit scientific journals, is the page charge. The page charge, which nearly always is underwritten by the federal government, amounts to a public subsidizing of information origination.

This lack of reliance on circulation for funds by journals would seem to question the argument that information production and dissemination hinges on readers paying directly for what they read. Moreover, because a majority of nonprofit journal publishers still appear to believe that photocopying encourages their circulations (although this view may be in a process of change), copying technologies would appear, in general, to benefit the dissemination of information as it is circulated in periodicals. What the preceding studies do not analyze are the economic effects of photocopying on copyright users. Nevertheless, photocopying has benefits, and some costs, for users, although these are not easily quantified.

Librarians, in particular, have derived benefits from photocopying. The cost of circulating books, a function that includes replacing vandalized pages and lost volumes, can account from 20 to 50 percent of a library's budget. Presumably, photocopying can reduce this portion of the librarian's budget because it reduces the need to circulate volumes and provides a substitute for the razoring out of pages by patrons. A survey conducted at the University of British Columbia indicated that 3.5 percent of the 181 library's patron queried admitted they would "steal or tear out the wanted pages" if photocopying machines were unavailable.

How much the emergence of photocopying has contributed to useful research and man's understanding of himself and the world is difficult (to say the least) to measure. It is known, however, that some kinds of scholarship, usually that which involves rare books, could not be accomplished without photocopying. As an example, Charles W. Shilling, Director of the George Washington University Biological Sciences Communications Project, has assembled a team that is trying to compile complete, annotated bibliographies of the literature on the baboon and chimpanzee. The project involves "xeroxing all the world's literature in this particular field," a task that "could definitely not be accomplished, no matter how much time and money was available" without photocopies. The team often has relied on a single copy of books which served as the only source in the United States.

An intriguing question to pose in this regard is: Which would suffer most, research or publishing, if photocopying were not available? The question is, of course, not easily answered, but the survey taken at the University of British Columbia indicated that research and library budgets might be affected more adversely than publishers' profits. Of the photocopy users who were asked what they would do without photocopiers, 72 percent said they would copy by hand, 19 percent said they would forget the whole matter, 5.5 percent would attempt to purchase, and the remainder would rip out the desired pages.

Relying on the University of British Columbia's figures and recalling that sci-tech information is copied most heavily, we can derive an approximation of the costs involved by imagining a situation in which roughly three-quarters of the engineers who needed to photocopy a page or two, instead sat down and wrote the material by longhand. Assuming that an engineer's time is worth 15 dollars an hour in an ordinary industrial complex, it would be far more economical to have him photocopy at even a dollar a sheet, rather than painstakingly transcribe by hand.

On the other hand, the 5.5 percent of copyright users who would be willing to buy the original source in the absence of photocopying opportunities (presuming the source was available when needed, if it were available at all), might amount to a respectable increase in sales. Sales mean royalties, and royalties have been essential, on occasion, to an author's livelihood. As we have noted, Herman Wouk has observed that James Joyce and Thomas Wolfe were living from hand to mouth on small royalty checks even at the height of their popularity.

On a considerably broader plane, however, the vast majority of writers who are not quite so talented as a Joyce or a Wolfe tend to indulge in authorship while holding down a more mundane job that pays bills on a regular basis. A 1965 survey by the Authors Guild indicated that the average income that authors derived from writing was about $3,000 a year. An eight-to-five job was a necessity to nearly all the writers questioned, and teaching was one of the most preferred occupations. One might speculate from this and other indicators that authors of the ilk that Joyce, Wolfe, and Marx represented, men who dedicated their life to writing, are waning, and that intellectual creativity is becoming bureaucratized in businesses, laboratories, and universities on even the most humanistic levels.

Much of this bureaucratization of intellectual creativity already is occurring in the field of textbook writing. It is noteworthy, in this respect, that textbook authors are perhaps an underpaid lot. It was revealed during the 1973 Senate hearings on copyright law revision that the "typical textbook author" has an income of "well under" $20,000 a year, and that royalties from texts more often than not are split among several co-authors. A textbook author normally receives 10 percent of his book's sale price (occasionally 15 percent, if it sells well), so the typical academic author's income, including that derived from royalties, probably is not high.

Rather than banning photocopiers as a stratagem to increase royalties derived from copyrighted publications, an even more lucrative (and certainly more feasible) arrangement would be the establishment of a copyright clearinghouse. A copyright clearinghouse, in theory, could charge the user at the photocopier by recording what was copied. The clearinghouse would tally the number of times and pages an author's works were copied within a particular period, and reimburse him and his publisher accordingly from the charges collected by the photocopying machines. A variant of this procedure would be to run periodic checks of what kinds of material were being copied, and in what proportion to total copying. Authors and publishers would be paid royalties collected at copying machines in accordance with the category of literature to which they contributed.

At first glance, such a scheme sounds horrendous in terms of equity among data-producers and administrative headaches. A copyright clearinghouse would require dimes to collect pennies; it reeks of "administrivia." On second glance, however, a copyright clearinghouse is quite plausible particularly when one considers the administrative potential of computer technology, and the use and distribution of photocopying machines in the United States. The CICP survey notes that most published material is copied in libraries, and the 1971 Canadian study indicates that 60.4 percent of all material copied in university libraries is owned by the library. Hence, the 15,500 public school systems with centralized libraries and the 22,500 remaining libraries in this country offer an existing, coherent system for administering in conjunction with a copyright clearinghouse. Certainly the American library system is at least as organized as are U.S. radio stations, which are subject currently to parallel regulations under the administration of the American Society of Composers, Authors, and Publishers.

Nevertheless, the costs of a clearinghouse, whatever its structure, are high. If it is based on individual subscriptions, annual costs could reach $300 million. A theoretically minimal cost of $10 million is possible, but this still could inhibit the dissemination of written works far more effectively than the possible loss of a few royalty payments. In short, a copyright clearinghouse could boost the transaction costs (i.e., the administrative costs incurred in obtaining permission from an owner to copy his product) inherent to any copyright policy. Presently, transaction costs are low, regulated largely by market mechanisms and by free access to photocopiers. With a clearinghouse, such costs easily might soar.

In summation, the economics of photocopying, while unclear in several respects, indicates that the financial incentive to write has not been affected measurably by copying machines. Nor have publishing houses in general suffered any perceptible monetary losses because of photocopying. Conversely, research costs may have been reduced by photocopying, a factor that should promote information production. But it should be reiterated that this situation is not static, and it is the potential use of photocopying more than any other single factor that concerns copyright owners. These observations apply at least equally strongly to other neopublishing technologies.

COMPUTERS AND COPYRIGHT

Computer-based information storage and retrieval systems comprise the second major economic and technological challenge to copyright as a public policy for intellectual creativity and the dissemination of ideas. The legal complexities of copyright and computers are enormous. When the problem was first recognized, in the early to mid-1960s, the entanglements were of such a novel character that a number of participants in copyright revision echoed the frustration of one lawyer who asked, "and not facetiously — whether the performance of a copyrighted computer program in a public showroom . . . constitutes a public performance . . . I would like to ask clarification . . . of what was intended with respect to copyrighted works in relation to their use in information storage and retrieval units."

So novel, in fact, was the role of information storage and retrieval systems that the Register of Copyrights admitted that in the 1964 Copyright Revision Bill, "we deliberately avoided any specific references to 'computers' or 'information storage and retrieval units' . . . we think it is safer to draft general language, which can be interpreted by the courts to apply to particular usages."

Bella L. Linden, then counsel for the American Textbook Publishers Institute, was among the first to analyze in detail the implications of information storage and retrieval systems for the copyright concept. Gipe states that with her words "Bella Linden changed the focus of the 1965 copyright revision hearings." Perhaps Gipe's contention is overstated. The Ad Hoc Task Group on Legal Aspects Involved in National Information Systems, of the Committee on Scientific and Technical Information (COSATI), Federal Council for Science and Technology, accurately noted that the "subject of information storage was only briefly considered by the House Committee at its Hearings on H.R. 4347 in 1965," and that no "testimony was offered by any governments agency on the impact of the proposed copyright revision on the computer usage of copyrighted material" in the 1967 hearings. Computers as an issue for copyright also were ignored during the Senate hearings in 1973.

Computer-manipulation of information may be categorized according to three processes: input, scanning, and output. Each one of these processes involves a potential infringement of copyright, although infringements must be defined in a context that might have appeared quite bizarre to the original framers of the 1909 Act.

Input, or feeding information into a system, requires the translation of data into a computer language in order to record it on cards or tapes, e.g., information written on survey research forms in English must be translated into numeric codes before the computer can use it. Since translation of a work is the legal prerogative of the copyright proprietor, an infringement may be evident when copyrighted data are encoded on punch cards or tapes.

Scanning, or the means by which the system reviews and retrieves data stored in its memory banks, also holds a potential danger of copyright infringement. It is possible that scanning might be the exclusive prerogative of the copyright owner of the information scanned, in that scanning data might be comparable to a performing right. In other words, the computer system is giving a performance using copyrighted data without the permission of the copyright owner.

Output involves a "republishing" of the computer system's data. When a computer user programs a system, which stores copyrighted data, to yield certain kinds of information, her or she may be creating a new anthology of copyrighted works that is "published" by the computer. Merely because information is assembled electronically on viewing screens or printouts, rather than printed in conventionally bound books, does not render the information any less free from copyright restrictions. Sophistication of format is no escape from copyright.

The 1974 Copyright Revision Bill (S. 1361) affects computer-based information storage and retrieval systems in that, in certain instances, the Bill could require researchers to secure permission from copyright owners in order to use their materials in computer runs. The point still is open to legal interpretation but, in cases where the judicial doctrine of fair use is not applicable, computer users could be subject to copyright infringement suits. Copyright owners contend that their intellectual property would escape copyright law merely by being run through a computer prior to its distribution. Requiring permissions from users at the input stage of a computer project would discourage this.

There are several arguments that can be voiced in behalf of the copyright owners' case concerning copyright control of input. One is that copyrighted input material is very likely to be reproduced in its entirety as the end-product of a computer run. Rather, such data probably would be produced by a computer system selectively, such as in providing answers to test questions, and thus likely would be subject to protection from infringement suits under the judicial doctrine of fair use (discussed in the following chapter). This argument concludes, therefore, that the sales of copyrighted works might decline.

The preceding argument is the principal contention of copyright owners relative to copyright control at the input stage of computer runs. Other arguments revolve around the cases of works with limited sales potentiality, such as scientific monographs (i. e., unless compensation is paid at input, scant royalties will be garnered by those publications seldom used by computer users because, while only one copy of the publication need be purchased by a computer system, libraries connected with that system might otherwise buy more copies than if they were not connected with the system); that is easier to control the input stage of the computer process than the output stage, because a copyright owner may be unable to calculate how many times his works have been reproduced as computer outputs; and that the copyright owner is better able to discourage distortion of his works at the input stage than at the output stage (we consider the distortion argument in greater detail in terms of the public domain policy in the following chapter).

Arguments against copyright control of input appear to be more persuasive than are those waged for it. One is that because some material may be rarely used by the system's users, the system's owners will never be able to recoup the initial costs of paying for copyrigh permissions at the input stage, hence control of output is relatively more desirable and reasonable. Another argument is that a permissions requirement on computer input could hamper scholarly research. Anthony G. Oettinger, Director of Harvard University Computer Center, has objected in congressional testimony that,

> I would have not only to acquire and evaluate materials, but in each instance, before experimenting with them, seek out the owner of a copyright, if any, make formal requests for permission to use the material, pay royalties . . . etc. All this before any material could actually be used and, in fact, before I could find out whether or not the material was useful! The delays, the frustrations and the chaos inherent in such a process now seem so formidable that . . . I would be tempted to return to the safer occupation of copying out manuscripts with a goose quill pen.

Some additional objections to control of the input stage include those that involve the potentiality, in effect, of paying double royalties to copyright owners. For instance, should it be decided by policymakers that both input and output should be subject to copyright, then users would be paying twice for use of the same material. Or, in the case of computer data-sharing arrangements, copyrighted material transferred from one machine to another might be charged two input fees for the transfer.

Finally, charges at the input stage may have some adverse effects on nonprofit educational institutions. The Interuniversity Communications Council, an organization of universities with interests in information technology, was the first users' group to call attention to the fact that, by requiring a copyright toll at the input stage of a computer run, certain exemptions for nonprofit institutions could be destroyed. Section 110(1) of the 1974 Bill exempts from copyright infringement suits the "display of a work by instructors or pupils in the course of face-to-face teaching . . . " To place a copyright toll at the input stage might abrogate this exemption, as the clauses may well be mutually conflicting.

Copyright control of output by computers also is being contemplated, i.e., can a computer printout of a copyrighted passage constitute an infringement of copyright? Involved in output-related issues are questions concerning display and fair use.

The present law grants the copyright owner the exclusive right to display his nondramatic literary work. Section 1 states that the owner may "exhibit, represent, produce, or reproduce" such works "in any manner or by any method whatsoever" and the proposed law gives the owner the exclusive right "to display the copyrighted work publicly." Nevertheless, the scanning process that is part of the internal operations of the computer may be considered a display that is legally subject to the control of the copyright owner. In 1967, a conscientious report by the House of Representatives stated that "the mere scanning or manipulation" of copyrighted data recorded in a computer should not be considered a violation of copyright, but S. 1361 tends to skirt the display issue as it pertains to computers.

Secondly, when a computer ultimately disgorges its output, it would be subject to possible copyright infringement suits. If printouts or viewing screens replicated sizeable amounts of copyrighted data already stored in its memory banks, then it might be a violation of copyright. "It" is an interesting word in this context. In terms of computer output, who or what would be "responsible?" The programmer? The program? The printout? Or the computer itself? In computer operations, these distinctions can become blurred.

A second and related aspect of copyright extending to computer usage of information refers to the registration of computer programs in the Copyright Office. The 1974 Copyright Revision Bill defines copyright in terms that may be adequately broad to include computer programs, depending on subsequent interpretation by the courts. Section 102(a) states that copyright protection "subsists . . . in original works of authorship fixed in any tangible medium of expression, now known or later developed, from which they can be perceived, reproduced, or otherwise communicated, either directly or with aid of a machine or device."

A computer program may be defined as instructions that set a computer's switches in order that it can function in a particular way. There are three kinds of programs: systems programs which control the operations of the machinery itself (e.g., Common Business Oriented Language, or COBOL), application programs which solve particular problems (e.g., the various programs used by scientists), and utility programs which can be used by a variety of users (e.g., a debugging program that corrects mistakes in other programs).

The question of registering computer programs is a hazy issue. The issue arose when John F. Banzhaf, III, wrote a program for law research in 1964, and decided to protect it. He discovered that the U.S. Patent Office had ruled computer programs could not be patented and eventually secured the first copyright for a computer program. Banzhaf and other copyright users contend that copyright protects the effort required to compile some kinds of programs, not the program's idea, and that copyright thus provides motivation to produce computer programs by distributing its cost among its users.

Since 1964, when the first copyright for a computer program was registered, only 200 programs had been registered by late 1970. This low number indicates that program developers find copyright unsuited to their needs. There are several reasons for this. One is that systems programs, such as COBOL, frequently are sold by computer manufacturers as part of their sales package, and development costs are absorbed in those sales. Secondly, application programs which, by definition, must be written in accordance with a particular user's needs, account for about 60 percent of all program development costs. These individually-tailored programs are hardly compatible with mass-oriented copyright concepts. Finally, utility programs, which one might think should derive the greatest benefit from copyright, are accompanied by expensive supporting items, such as documentation annuals, debugging arrangements, and periodical hardware adjustments that are made for the individual client. The cost of these supporting items often equals or exceeds the cost of the original utility program, a fact that tends to undercut the applicability of copyright to even these relatively mass-oriented computer programs. While it seems possible that copyright protection might be appropriate for generally usable, off-the-shelf low-priced programs that are sold separately from computer hardware and to widely dispersed buyers (who would unlikely to find it practical to agree on time-sharing arrangements), copyright does not now appear to be a public policy that benefits the distribution of information as it is formatted in most computer programs.

Overall, what are the advantages and disadvantages of copyright protection of computer-based data and computer programs? The advantages of copyright protection seem reasonably straightforward. One such advantage is that registering a work in the Copyright Office is simple and cheap, which is not the case in patent registration, and which has been proposed as an alternative to copyright protection of computer programs. Also, under copyright law, once infringement is proven, a copyright owner can collect damages even though no actual damage is demonstrated.

These advantages of copyright protection of computer systems are predicated on the notion that such protection of the program developer is indeed desirable as a public policy because it facilitates the growth and use of knowledge. Similarly, many of the disadvantages of copyright as a public policy for computers are premised on the same presumption. For example, copyright, as we indicated earlier, does not protect the original idea behind the program. Rather, copyright as a concept prohibits only the outright copying of the program and not the originality, creativeness, and inventiveness of the program's designer, as patent protection is designed to do. Secondly, copyright protection probably would not protect against a computer using the program. This notion relates to the judicial doctrine of fair use, described in the following chapter, but more directly to a related court-created idea. In 1880, the U.S. Supreme Court ruled in Baker v. Seldon that the "methods and diagrams" used in an art book for purposes of showing the reader how to improve his art were not protected by copyright. Such techniques were "necessary incidents to the art, and given therewith to the public," because they were used "for the purpose of practical application." This decision still stands, and in 1967 the Deputy Register of Copyrights relied on it in explaining copyright and the computer-use of computer programs. "If you had a copyrighted program, which somebody finds it necessary to use, such use is not an infringement." Finally, policing the use computer programs, as with the photocopying of copyrighted works, is extremely difficult. In both cases, technology has skipped away from the cumbersome authority of the state.

The advantages and disadvantages of copyright as it relates to computers that we have reviewed are practical ones, i.e., they implicitly assume that some kind of public control is needed over the use of computer programs. There is a far more fundamental issue: Should information needed for computer manipulation of knowledge be limited at all? Copyright, after all, was not designed with computers in mind. In an extensive study of copyright and computers, an Ad Hoc Task Group of the Council on Scientific and Technical Information of the Federal Council for Science and Technology observed that "copyright may hinder the maximum efficient use of national information systems." The effects of such hindrances would squelch the growth of information systems within the disciplines, perhaps render illegal abstracts of articles now used in information systems, and delay inclusion, or possibly exclude, some information from systems even after the copyright owner is contacted.

More significantly, perhaps, the copyright appears to be growing increasingly irrelevant to the actual and practical development of computer-based information systems. In an interview published in Publishers' Weekly in 1973, John Price, director of Exxon Corporation's sophisticated information center, stated that publishers should solve the theoretical and technical problems of transmitting single-copy volumes over long distances "before worrying so much about the legalities of copyright." Price, for example, has not worried about such legalities, and is a managerial leader in the business of business information. He believes, and possibly rightly, that publishers "are going to have to restructure their ways to doing business" in light of the new technologies and the new patterns of informational needs and use.

CONCLUSION

In this chapter we have reviewed the economies and social dynamics of the copyright principle, publishing trade, photocopying practices, and computer-based information storage and retrieval systems. As we have noted, these phenomena become increasingly blurred entities as new technologies and informational patterns proliferate, but it stands that the copyright concept, as the sole public policy for the creation and distribution of knowledge in this country, determines to a significant degree past, present, and future patterns of knowledge in our technological culture. In the following chapter, we consider how copyright has been circumvented by government and society in a practical attempt to enhance the growth of knowledge in American society.

REFERENCES

Alpert, D. and Bitzer, D. L. (1970). Advances in computer-based education. Science CLXVII, March 20, 1582-1590.

American Textbook Publishers Institute and the American Book Publishers Council (1966). An economic-media study of book publishing. New York: The American Textbook Publishers Institute and the American Book Publishers Council.

Arts Council of Great Britain (1968). The arts council and public lending right. London: The Arts Council of Great Britain, January.

Beer, Stafford (1970). "Managing Modern Complexity." The management of information and knowledge. A compilation of papers prepared for the Eleventh Meeting of the Panel on Science and Technology, Committee on Science and Astronautics, U.S. House of Representatives. Washington: U.S. Government Printing Office, 41-62.

Benjamin, Curtis G. (1971). A Publisher's Viewpoint—Profit Seeking. In Encyclopedia of library and information science (Volume 6), Allen Kent and Harold Lancour (Eds.). New York: Marcel Dekker, Inc., 82-86.

Benjamin, Curtis G. (1966). Computers and copyrights. Science CLII, April 8, 181-194.

Benjamin, Curtis G. (1966). Copyright and Government. Library Journal XCI, February 15, 881-886.

Benjamin, Curtis G. (1974). Letters. Science 184, May 10, 610.

Benjamin, Curtis G. (1974). Soaring prices and sinking sales of science monographs. Science 183, January 25, 282-284.

Blackburn, Robert H. (1970). Photocopying in a university library. Scholarly Publishing II, October, 49-58.

Breyer, Stephen (1970). The uneasy case for copyright: A study of copyright in books, photocopies, and computer programs. Harvard Law Review LXXXIV, December, 281-351.

Brown, George W., Miller, James G., and Keenan, Thomas A. (Eds.) (1967). EDUNET. Report of the Summer Study on Information Networks Conducted by the Interuniversity Communications Council (EDUCOM). New York: John Wiley and Sons, Inc., XIX, p. 440.

Brown, Ralph S., Jr. (1969). Appendix: Copyright problems of research libraries. In On research libraries. Statement and recommendations of the Committee on Research Libraries of the American Council of Learned Societies. Submitted to the National Advisory Commission on Research Libraries, November, 1967. Cambridge, Massachusetts: The M.I.T. Press, 86-100.

Brown, Ralph S., Jr. (1971). Property rights under the new technology. In Computers, communications, and the public interest, Martin Greenberger (Ed.). Baltimore, Maryland: The John Hopkins Press, 189-206.

Brudner, Harvey J. (1968). Computer-managed instruction. Science 162, November 29, 970-976.

Burke, John Emmett (1966). The rising tide — more research libraries. Commerce, Texas: East Texas State University, V, p. 293.

Bush, George P. (1972). Technology and copyright: An annotated bibliography and source materials. Mt. Airy, Maryland: Lomond Systems, Inc.

Busha, Charles H. and Landrum, John H. (1967). Telefacsimile communication with the Xerox Magnavox Telecopier in reference to interlibrary loans: A report of a three-month experimental demonstration conducted by the South Carolina State Library Board. Columbia, South Carolina: South Carolina State Library Board, July, 27.

Cambridge Research Institute (1973). Omnibus Copyright Revision: Analysis of the Issues, Arthur B. Hanson (Ed.). Washington: American Society for Information Science.

Clapp, Verner W. (1968). Copyright — a librarian's view. Prepared for the National Advisory Commission on Libraries. Washington: Copyright Committee, Association of Research Libraries.

Clarke, Robert F. (1963). The impact of photocopying on scholarly publishing. Library Journal LXXXVIII, July, 2625-2629.

Council of Economic Advisers (1970). Economic report of the President, 1970. Washington, D.C.: U.S. Government Printing Office.

Deighton, Lee C. (1966). Statement. In Copyright law revision. Hearings before Subcommittee No. 3 of the Committee on the Judiciary, House of Representatives, 89th Cong., 1st Sess., on H.R. 4347, H.R. 5680, H.R. 6835. May 26, 1965. Serial No. 8. Part 1. Washington: U.S. Government Printing Office, 66-71.

Dessauer, John H. (1969). Statement. In Establish a select senate committee on technology and the human environment. Hearings before the Subcommittee on Intergovernmental Relations of the Committee on Government Operations, United States Senate, 91st Cong., 1st Sess., on S. Res. 78. March 5, 1969. Washington: U.S. Government Printing Office, 149-153.

Dessauer, John P. (1973). Where the book buyers' money goes. Publishers' Weekly 204, July 30, 42-43.

Duggan, Michael A. (1971). The viewpoint of the computer scientist. In Encyclopedia of library and information science (Volume 6), Allen Kent and Harold Lancour (Eds.). New York: Marcel Dekker, Inc., 99-136.

Ennis, Philip, with Schlipf, Frederick A. (1966). Copying and Duplicating in American Education. A report of surveys undertaken by the National Opinion Research Council, An economic-media study of book publishing. New York: The American Textbook Publishers Institute and the American Book Publishers Council, 166-283.

Federal Council for Science and Technology (1967). Committee on Scientific and Technical Information. Ad Hoc Task Group on Legal Aspects Involved in National Information Systems. The copyright law as it relates to national information systems and national programs. A study by the Ad Hoc Task Group on Legal Aspects Involved in National Information Systems, PB-175 618, July, 1967. Washington: U.S. Government Printing Office.

Fisher, Arthur (1960). The copyright office: Report to the Librarian of Congress by the Register of Copyrights. Annual report of the Librarian of Congress for the fiscal year ending June 30, 1959. Washington: U.S. Government Printing Office, 72-84.

George Fry and Associates (1962). Survey of copyrighted material reproduction practices in scientific and technical fields. Study prepared for the National Science Foundation. Chicago: George Fry and Associates.

Gipe, George A. (1967). Nearer to the dust: Copyright and the machine. Baltimore: Williams and Wilkins Press.

Goldman, Abe A. (1964). The concept of the law of copyright. In Reprography and copyright law, Lowell H. Hattery and George P. Bush (Eds.). Baltimore, Maryland: Port City Press, Inc., 11-17.

Goldman, Abe A. (1960). Study No. 1: The history of U.S.A. copyright law revision from 1901 to 1954. July, 1955. In Copyright law revision. Studies prepared for the Subcommittee on Patents, Trademarks, and Copyrights of the Committee on the Judiciary, United States Senate, 86th Cong., 1st Sess. Pursuant to S. Res. 53. Studies 1-4. Washington: U.S. Government Printing Office, IX-XI.

Gosnell, Charles F. (1966). The copyright grab-bag: Observations on the new copyright legislation. ALA Bulletin LX, January, 46-55.

Grannis, Chandler B. (1973). AAP annual statistics. Publishers' Weekly 204, July 30, 38-40.

Greenberger, Martin (Ed.) (1971). Computers, communications, and the public interest. Baltimore, Maryland: The Johns Hopkins Press.

Hattery, Lowell H. and Bush, George P. (Eds.) (1969). Reprography and copyright law. Baltimore, Maryland: Port City Press, Inc.

Heilprin, Lawrence B. (1967). Technology and the Copyright Principle. Phi Delta Kappan XLVIII, January, 220-225.

Henry, Nicholas L. (1974). Copyright, public policy, and information technology. Science 183, February 1, 384-391.

Janeway, Elizabeth (1967). Statement. In Copyright law revision. Hearings before the Subcommittee on Patents, Trademarks, and Copyrights of the Committee on the Judiciary, United States Senate, 90th Cong., 1st Sess. Pursuant to S. Res. 37 on S. 597, Part 1, March 15, 1967. Washington: U.S. Government Printing Office, 33-37.

Joint Libraries Committee on Fair Use in Photocopying (1961). Report on single copies. Special Libraries LII, May/June, 251-255.

Kaminstein, Abraham L. (1965). Copyright law revision, Part 5. 1964 revision bill with discussions and comments, 89th Cong., 1st Sess., September, 1965. Washington: U.S. Government Printing Office.

Kaminstein, Abraham L. (1969). The Copyright Office. Annual report of the Libraries of Congress for the fiscal year ending June 30, 1968. Washington: U.S. Government Printing Office, 68-89.

Koepke, John C. (1964). Assessment of Documentation Practices in Reprography. In Reprography and copyright law, Lowell H. Hattery and George P. Bush (Eds.). Baltimore, Maryland: Port City Press, Inc., 1964; 50-58.

Lamberton, D. M. (Ed.) (1971). Economics of information and knowledge: Selected readings. Middlesex: Penguin Books.

Lieb, Charles H. (1967). The computer and copyright: The next five years. Publishers' Weekly CXCII, September 18, 40-42.

Linden, Bella L. (1967). Statement. In Copyright law revision. Hearings before the Subcommittee on Patents, Trademarks, and Copyrights of the Committee on the Judiciary, United States Senate, 90th Cong., 1st Sess. Pursuant to S. Res. 37 on S. 597, Part 4, April 28, 1967. Washington: U.S. Government Printing Office, 1063-1065.

Loeb, Rhoades, and Co. (1965). Book publishing and federal aid to education. New York: Loeb, Rhoades, and Co.

Machlup, Fritz (1962). The production and distribution of knowledge in the United States. Princeton, New Jersey: Princeton University Press.

Madison, James (1961). No. 43. In The federalist papers, Clinton Rossiter (Ed.). New York: The New American Library, 271-280.

Marke, Julius J. (1967). Copyright and intellectual property. New York: The Fund for the Advancement of Education.

Markham, Jesse W. (1966). An economic analysis of the new information technologies. An economic-media study of book publishing. New York: The American Textbook Publishers Institute and the American Book Publishers Council, 1-27.

Markham, Jesse W. (1967). Statement. In Copyright law revision. Hearings before the Subcommittee on Patents, Trademarks, and Copyrights of the Committee on the Judiciary, United States Senate, 90th Cong., 1st Sess. Pursuant to S. Res. 37 on S. 597, Part 1, March 15, 1967. Washington: U.S. Government Printing Office, 64-73.

Massachusetts Institute of Technology (1969). Project INTREX. PB-183 138. Cambridge, Massachusetts: M.I.T., September 15.

Mathews, Max V. and Brown W. Stanley (1969). Research libraries and the new technology. In On research libraries. Statement and recommendations of the Committee on Research Libraries of the Committee on Research Libraries of the American Council of Learned Societies. Submitted to the National Advisory Commission on Research Libraries, November, 1967. Cambridge, Massachusetts: The M.I.T. Press, 59-76.

McColough, C. Peter (1966). Speech to the Los Angeles Society of Financial Analysts, June 3, 1965. Quoted in Bella L. Linden. Statement. In Copyright law revision. Hearings before Subcommittee No. 3 of the Committee on the Judiciary, House of Representatives, 89th Cong., 1st Sess., on H.R. 4347, H.R. 5680, H.R. 6831, H.R. 6835. June 30, 1965. Serial No. 8, Part 3. Washington: U.S. Government Printing Office, p. 1430.

Morehouse, H. G. (1966). Telefacsimile services between libraries with the Xerox Magnavox Telecopier. Sponsored by the Council on Library Resources, Inc., Washington, D.C., Report No. CLR-314. Reno, Nevada: University of Nevada Library, December 20.

Nimmer, Melville B. (1968). Project: New technology and the law of copyright: Reprography and computers. UCLA Law Review XV, April, 931-1030.

Oettinger, Anthony G. with Marks, Sema (1969). Run, computer, run: The mythology of educational innovation. Cambridge, Massachusetts: Harvard University Press.

Oettinger, Anthony G. (1967). Statement. In Copyright law revision. Hearings before the Subcommittee on Patents, Trademarks, and Copyrights of the Committee on the Judiciary, United States Senate, 90th Cong., 1st Sess. Pursuant to S. Res. 37 on S. 597, Part 2, April 4, 1967. Washington: U.S. Government Printing Office, 581-589.

Overhage, Carl F. J. and Harmon, R. Joyce (Eds.) (1965). INTREX: Report of a planning conference on information transfer experiments. September 3, 1965. Sponsored by the Independence Foundation of Philadelphia, Pennsylvania. Cambridge: Massachusetts: The M.I.T. Press.

Palmour, Vernon E., Bryant, Edward C., Caldwell, Nancy W., and Gray, Lucy M. (Compilers) (1972). A study of the characteristics, costs, and magnitude of interlibrary loans in academic libraries. Westport, Connecticut: Greenwood Publishing Co.

Palmour, Vernon E. (1974). Letters. Science 184, May 10, 609-610.

Pforzheimer, Walter L. (1964). Historical perspective on copyright law and fair use. In Reprography and copyright law, Lowell H. Hattery and George P. Bush (Eds.). Baltimore, Maryland: Port City Press, Inc., 18-35.

Platt, John Rader (1966). The step to man. New York: John Wiley and Sons.

Price, Miles O. (1960). Photocopying by libraries: A precis. Library Trends VIII, January, 442-444.

Reeding, M. Frank (1963). Revolution in the textbook publishing industry. Occasional Paper No. 9. A report prepared for the Technological Development Project of the National Education Association of the United States. Washington: Department of Audiovisual Instruction, National Education Association.

Reville, Charles O., Jr. (1973). Pricing, licensing, microform publishing, and copyright as a source of income: The commercial publishers. Economics of scientific publications, Council of Biology Editors (Eds.). Washington: Council of Biology Editors, 6-12.

Roberts, Matt (1969). Copyright and photocopying: An experiment in cooperation. College and research libraries XXX, May, 222-229.

Rosenfield, Harry N. (1967). Statement. In Copyright law revision. Hearings before the Subcommittee on Patents, Trademarks, and Copyrights of the Committee on the Judiciary, United States Senate, 90th Cong., 1st Sess. Pursuant to S. Res. 37 on S. 597, Part 4, April 28, 1967. Washington: U.S. Government Printing Office, 1043-1053.

Rossiter, Clinton (Ed.) (1961). The federalist papers. New York: The New American Library.

Schieber, William D. and Schoffner, Ralph M. (1968). Telefacsimile in libraries—a report of an experiment in facsimile transmission and an analysis of implications for interlibrary loan systems. Berkeley, California: University of California at Berkeley, Institute of Library Research, February.

Shilling, Charles W. (1967). Letter of April 28, 1967 to the Ad Hoc Task Group of COSATI. Quoted in Federal Council for Science and Technology. Committee on Scientific and Technical Information. Ad Hoc Task Group on Legal Aspects Involved in National Information Systems. The copyright law as it relates to national information systems and programs. A Study by the Ad Hoc Task Group on Legal Aspects Involved in National Information Systems, PB-175 618, July, 1967. Washington: U.S. Government Printing Office, p. 49.

Society of Authors (1968). Public lending right: Outline of proposals, 1968. London: The Society of Authors.

Society of Authors and the Publishers Association (1965). Photocopying and the law: A guide for librarians and teachers and other suppliers and users of photocopies of copyright works. London: Strand Press Service, Ltd.

Sophar, Gerald J. and Heilprin, Laurence B. (1967). The determination of legal facts and economic guideposts with respect to the dissemination of scientific and educational information as it is affected by copyright—a status report. Final Report: Project No. 7-0793, Contract No. OEC-1-7-070793-3559. Committee to Investigate Copyright Problems Affecting Communication in Science and Education, Inc. Washington: U.S. Department of Health, Education, and Welfare, Office of Education, Bureau of Research, December.

Stuart-Stubbs, B. (1971). Purchasing and copying practices at Canadian university libraries: Two studies performed for the Association of College and University Libraries Committee on Copyright Legislation. Ottawa: Canadian Library Association.

Technology vs. copyright: Form vs. content. (1969). Publishers' Weekly CXCVI, August 11, 18-20.

Teplitz, Arthur (1970). Microfilm and reprography. Annual review of information science and technology: Volume 5, 1970, Carlos A. Cuadra and Ann W. Luke (Eds.). American Society for Information Science. Chicago: William Benton, Publisher, 87-111.

U.S. Congress (1966). House. Committee on the Judiciary. Copyright law revision. Report No. 2237 to Accompany H.R. 4347, 89th Cong., 2nd Sess. October 12, 1966. Washington: U.S. Government Printing Office.

U.S. Congress (1967). House. Committee on the Judiciary. Copyright law revision. Report No. 83 to Accompany H.R. 2512, 90th Cong., 1st Sess. March 8, 1967. Washington: U.S. Government Printing Office, 254.

Yerkes, Charles P. (1964). Interests of the copying-machine industry. In Reprography and Copyright Law, Lowell H. Hattery and George P. Bush (Eds.). Baltimore, Maryland: Port City Press, Inc., 69-76.

Walden, K. E. (1955). Common law rights in literary property. Journal of the Patent Office Society XXXVII, September, 642-659.

Williams, Edwin E. (1969). Bibliographical control and physical dissemination. In On research libraries. Statement and recommendations of the Committee on Research Libraries of the American Council of Learned Societies. Submitted to the National Advisory Commission on Research Libraries, November, 1967. Cambridge, Massachusetts: The M.I.T. Press, 26-58.

Wouk, Herman (1966). Statement. In Copyright law revision. Hearings before Subcommittee No. 3, Committee on the Judiciary, United States House of Representatives, 89th Cong., 1st Sess., Serial No. 8. Part 1. May 28, 1965. Washington: U.S. Government Printing Office, 110-113.

Chapter 4

COPYRIGHT: UMBRAGES AND OPTIONS

In the last two chapters we have been dwelling on the potential dysfunctions of the copyright concept in our technological culture. One might conclude from those discussions that public policymakers lived in a world of blissful obsolescence, neither knowing of nor caring about the changing informational patterns in the society swirling about them. Such a conclusion would be erroneous, however, because, over the years, policymakers in all three branches of the national government have, in effect, taken umbrage at the copyright concept as an adequate policy for promoting science and the useful arts. The executive branch has questioned copyright with its public domain policy, the legislative branch has evolved its not-for-profit principle, and the judicial branch has created the fair use doctrine.

We consider these exceptions in turn and review some modifications of and alternatives to copyright that hold some potentiality for being more responsive to the new information technologies.

THE DYSFUNCTIONS OF COPYRIGHT: THREE OFFICIAL RECOGNITIONS

The Executive "Public Domain" Policy

The most outstanding of these recognitions that copyright may no longer be adequate as a public policy for knowledge management is expressed in Section 8 of the present Copyright Act, which states that "No copyright shall subsist . . . in any publication of the United States Government, or any reprint, in whole or in part . . . " This clause amounts to exempting all U.S. Government publications from copyright restrictions on the ground that such publications are in the public domain.

The exemption is continued in Section 105 of the present revision bill, which states that "Copyright protection . . . is not available for any work of the United States Government, but the . . . Government is not precluded from receiving and holding copyrights transferred to it by assignment, bequest, or otherwise."

This clause was not always in U.S. copyright laws. Traditionally, it was assumed that federal publications were in the public domain. It was at the turn of the century when Congressman James D. Richardson compiled a book entitled Messages and Papers of the Presidents, and printed it at government expense under his own copyright, Washington's Farewell and Lincoln's Gettysburg addresses were included. Richardson earned $11,320 in royalties, and in the process, initiated a Senate investigation which concluded that "the law as it stands is sufficient to deny copyright to any and every work once issued as a government publication." Nevertheless, it was thought prudent to state this point explicitly when the law was revised in 1909.

Recognition by the copyright law itself that copyright is, in instances of documents in the public domain, a policy not in the public interest serves as a remarkably candid statement on the part of policymakers relative to the inadequacy of copyright as an information policy. A panel of leading editors and scholars noted a few years ago that the "Federal Government is today the major source of information in practically every field of endeavor," emphasizing what we already have documented in the first chapter: The exemption of publicly sponsored information from copyright restraints is not a minor one.

Because the exemption is not small, pressure has been brought on policymakers to weaken its applicability. In 1965, the U.S. Office of Education (USOE) took a strong stand on the right of government to deprive copyright status from works it had funded by inserting in the Federal Register a ruling that stated: "Material produced as a result of any research activity undertaken with any financial assistance through contract with or project grant from the Office of Education will be placed in the public domain [and] . . . will be available to conventional outlets of the private sector for their use."

The USOE statement affected a publishing industry of roughly $1 billion in magnitude, which is about what American schools spend annually on teaching materials. USOE itself regularly distributes about $100 million in research funds.

While the USOE policy did not represent a change in law, it did signify a change in fact. The Office of Education traditionally had permitted its researchers to copyright their products, although it also required the researcher to give the government a royalty-free license to use his work as it chose, and to authorize others to do so as well. Copyright was a frail instrument in these cases, but nevertheless was thought by some researchers and publishers to be worthwhile and binding. The new ruling changed this impression.

Publishers responded by arguing that copyrighting and commercially distributing works financed by taxpayers was indeed in the public interest because it expanded the works' audience, saved the taxpayers' money by placing distribution costs on private firms, increased the works' availability, and prevented the distortion of material.

The reasoning behind these arguments is not entirely clear. For example, the publishers' contention that copyrighted commercial publications would be more widely read than uncopyrighted government publications is not supportedby facts. Some of the all-time best sellers in America have been government documents: more than 13 million copies of Infant Care have been sold, 7.6 million copies of Your Federal Income Tax, 7.4 million copies of Prenatal Care, and 5.7 million copies of Your Child from One to Six. On the other hand, a best seller in commercial circles usually is defined as any book that sells more than 50,000 copies.

Moreover, publishers have made profits on uncopyrighted government documents without copyrighting their own versions. The Warren Commission's report (from which five publishing houses made money), the Surgeon General's report on smoking, the report of President's Commission on Civil Disorders, and the notorious Watergate transcripts are examples. A few years ago AMS Press announced that it was reprinting the thirty-nine volumes of congressional hearings on The Pearl Harbor Attack and the forty-two volumes of The Nuremberg Trials, both of which originally were published by the government but are now out of print. Respective prices for the buckram-bound sets will be \$1,890 (or nearly \$41 per book) and \$1,300 (or \$31 per book). Publishers hardly seem excluded from profits by the absence of copyright.

Publishers also contend that distribution of government-sponsored research through private firms saves public money. This argument assumes that the U.S. Government Printing Office oversees a losing operation, which it does not. Generally, the Government Printing Office makes a profit. In this connection, Senator Russell B. Long has observed that to reason the federal government should both finance the research and secure private profits by extending copyright protection to the same research "is tantamount to saying the Government should finance the building of highways and then permit private companies to charge tolls."

The argument that extending copyright protection to government research would increase the work's availability by providing firms an incentive to disseminate it seems particularly spurious. Copyright protection currently can endure on any single item for as long as fifty-six years, and thousands of successful law suits have been initiated by copyright owners against users who have tried to shorten that span of time. Many researchers enjoy copyright protection even though they never have had their writings distributed by publication.

In this vein, copyright is seen by some to be an effective censor of sensitive public documents. Major General C. G. Dodge, the Army's Chief of Information, has written that copyright has prevented the quotation of public material out of context, and thus is beneficial to the public interest in that it has discouraged such practices. Another way of phrasing this viewpoint (which generally is supported by copyright owners) is that officialdom may stop the public's use of public information if such use is inconvenient to particular bureacrats.

Dodge's statement leads to the final argument of publishers: Copyright prevents an author's ideas and material from being distorted by more shallow intellects. A more reasonable view would be that since no scholar can claim ultimate wisdom, tampering with his ideas is as likely to lead to beneficial as detrimental results. In any event, the fact that innovation is being encouraged due to the absence of copyright would seem sufficient cause to risk a few misrepresentations of research.

If the arguments of publishers against a public domain policy are less than water-tight, publishers nevertheless have been able to gain two legal victories. The first was a relatively minor concession by the Office of Education in 1968 which amounted to a somewhat more flexible doctrine on what kinds of government-funded research could be defined as being in the public domain. The new USOE statement says that exemptions to normal public domain criteria will be granted to works for which it can be shown that copyright offers essentially the only feasible route for getting the material published, and that USOE may limit the duraction of copyright according to its own judgement.

The second concession to owners was more substantial and is found in the definition of "a work of the U.S. Government," as defined in the Copyright Law Revision Bills appearing since 1967. Such a work is defined in Section 101 of the present bill as one "prepared by an officer or employee of the U.S. Government as part of his official duties." The definition omits reference to outside research funded in part by federal agencies, which accounts for roughly 85 percent of federal R & D activities.

While the USOE's modified public domain policy and the proposed definition of a work of the U.S. Government are concessions of some advantage to the friends of copyright, it nonetheless stands that the basic view of the federal establishment is anticopyright in terms of originating and disseminating information that is financed by taxpayers. This position was reaffirmed by the United States government in 1971 and in 1973. In 1971, the National Institutes of Health (NIH) announced in the Federal Register that "a policy change" with regard to copyright and research funding was being made, and in 1973 this change was modified and established. The NIH policy now holds that "any publication, film or other similar communication material developed or resulting from a project supported in whole or in part" by an NIH grant may be copyrighted by the author or by the journal publishing the research. But, such a copyright "is subject to a royalty-free, nonexclusive and irrevocable license or right in the government to reproduce, translate, publish, use, disseminate, and dispose of such material and to authorize others to do so." Additionally, NIH-funded research may be copied in single copies by individuals using "any means available to them, without regard to the copyright of the journal, and without royalty."

Such a policy represents a formidably anticopyright attitude on the part of the federal bureaucracy. Moreover, such a view possesses some logic and it affects the creation and distribution of a vast portion of information in society.

The Legislative "Not-for-Profit" Principle

A second official recognition that copyright is not always the optimal public policy toward publicly accessible information is the not-for-profit principle of the current Copyright Act. The not-for-profit limitation authorizes nonprofit, public performances of nondramatic literary and musical copyrighted materials without requiring the permission of the copyright owner. Educators long have assumed that the not-for-profit principle protected educational uses of copyrighted works from infringement suits. Although the Register of Copyrights recommended that the not-for-profit principle be retained, it has been deleted from the current Copyright Revision Bill as the result of an agreement in 1966 between copyright owners and users.

Nevertheless, despite the formal deletion by Congress of a not-for-profit principle in the present Revision Bill, the thinking that educational and scholarly activities should be protected from copyright-induced inhibitions is reflected in numerous other sections of the bill.

The Copyright Revision Bill of 1974 has clauses in it that specifically exempt a substantial portion of library photocopying from infringement suits; omit restrictions on student uses of information storage and retrieval systems; exclude instructors, librarians, and archivitsts who copy protected material in good faith from prosecution by copyright owners; give statutory recognition to the judicial doctrine of fair use; and establish a moratorium on copyright infringement suits involving information storage and retrieval systems until further study of new data technologies can be made. The reasoning behind all these clauses is that nonprofit uses of copyrighted information are involved, and they would seem to amount to a de facto (if not, perhaps, de jure) recognition by legislators of the traditional not-for-profit limitation so long a part of American copyright law.

A recent report published by the Senate Committee on the Judiciary explains this new thrust of the not-for-profit principle in the latest Copyright Law Revision Bill, S. 1361. Section 106(4) of the 1974 Bill is designed, in the words of the Report, "first to state the public performance right in broad terms, and then to provide specific exemptions for educational and other nonprofit uses. This approach is more reasonable than the outright exemption of the 1909 statute." These specific exemptions for educational and other nonprofit uses. This approach is more reasonable than the outright exemption of the 1909 statute." These specific exemptions are found in Section 110, Clauses (1) through (4) of the Bill.

Clauses (1) and (2) cover educational exemptions. Clause (1) exempts the display or performance of all types of copyrighted works e.g., computer display, photocopies) from infringement suits when such performances are given "by instructors or pupils in the course of face-to-face teaching activities of a nonprofit educational institution," where these activities occur "in a classroom or similar place devoted to instruction." Clause (2) exempts instructional broadcasts (with certain limitations) from infringement suits that use copyrighted works, Clause (3) affects works of a religious nature, and Clause (4) is "a general exception to the exclusive right of public performance that would cover some, though not all, of the same ground as the present 'for profit' limitations," i.e., public performances of nondramatic literary and musical works. It is a more restrictive clause than the present version, however, because the exemption would be limited to public performances given directly in the presence of an audience, although such performances could be given by nonhuman performers, such as a computer. In addition, no profit motive can be present, no direct or indirect payments may be charged for the performance, and any proceeds deriving from the performance cannot be used for private gain.

In sum, the proposed changes in the not-for-profit principle of the 1909 Act reflect a desire by legislators to protect private enterprises (particularly broadcasting corporations) from unfair competition, but overridingly to assure that nonprofit educational institutions are in no way restricted by copyright owners from using the new information technologies for the optional benefit of their students. The not-for-profit limitation is a major legislative exception to the copyright concept as a public policy for knowledge management, and its viability remains very current in policy-making circles.

The Adjudicative "Fair Use" Doctrine

A third recognition by policymakers that copyright arrangements do not facilitate the transmission of knowledge in all circumstances has come from the courts. The judicial doctrine of "fair use" is a powerful anticopyright tool, the origins of which can be traced back as far as 1841 in this country.

Fair use represents an effort on the part of the courts to ameliorate the effects of a literal interpretation of what the Copyright Act of 1909 says "copyright" means. The General Counsel of the Copyright Office characterizes fair use as a "'safety valve'" on rigidity of the law's definition of copyright. He observes that if "the author's exclusive rights were absolute, if they restricted every use of his work, then copyright could indeed become a road block to the growth and spread of learning and culture. To achieve the purposes stated in the Constitution, the works of authors must be made available for use by the public while, at the same time, the author enjoys such exclusive rights as will give him a just reward for his contribution to society."

No one ever has really defined fair use. It does not appear in the U.S. Copyright Law, but is simply (again in the words of the General Counsel), a result of "the necessity for interpreting the exclusive right to 'copy' as being subject to a rule of reason, without which copyright could become an intolerable restraint on the public's use of copyrighted material." The Register of Copyrights, in his 1961 Report on copyright law revision, stated that the "term eludes precise definition: broadly speaking, it means that a reasonable portion of a copyrighted work may be reproduced without permission when necessary for a legitimate purpose which is not competitive with the copyright owner's market for his work."

The Register also noted that to determine whether a specific use of a copyrighted work was fair use or infringement, the courts generally relied on four criteria: "(1) the purpose of the use, (2) the nature of the copyrighted work, (3) the amount and substantiality of the material used in relation to the copyrighted work as a whole, and (4) the effect of the use on the copyright owner's potential market for his work." While these bases ofjudicial decision may vary and interrelate, the fourth criterion, "the competitive character of the use," is often the most decisive.

How the doctrine of fair use affects users of information technologies, notably library and education interests, remains unclear. Borge Varmer, author of an early study on library photocopying commissioned by the Register of Copyrights, stated that "the justification for the photocopying of copyrighted material would seem to be sound on the doctrine of 'fair use'", a notion that the Register's Report echoes. Walter L. Pforzheimer, a trustee of the Yale University Library and a recognized authority on copyright law, takes a counterview. He argues that if "there is one thing which library photocopying is not, it is not fair use within any judicial usage of that doctrine." Furthermore, contends Pforzheimer, "the replication of copyrighted material as now practiced by libraries seems to be a violation of the Copyright Law, and in extreme cases carries severe overtones of unfair competition."

In terms of scholarly interests, it also has been argued that fair use justifies copying for educational purposes. The Register's Report of 1961 stated that "the general scope of fair use can be indicated by . . . Quotation of short passages in a scholarly or technical work . . . Reproduction by a teacher or student of a small part of a work to illustrate a lesson," among other examples. But, in conjunction with problems of library copying, authorities differ as to whether fair use has any relation to the scholarly use of copyrighted material. An observer who is at once a librarian, educator, and publisher asserts that fair use has no relation whatsoever with the private use of material, by which he means the copying of copyrighted material for research purposes. Private use is legitimate under copyright law, but should not be confused with the concept of public use of copyrighted works, which is included under the doctrine of fair use. Public use questions arise when material is copied and subsequently published to the extent that it is in unfair competition with the copyright owner.

Arguments revolving around whether fair use is or is not relevant to photocopying and other information technologies may prove not. Congress appears to act on the assumption that fair use is pertinent to photocopying, and has issued statements to that effect. Of particular interest in this regard are House Reports No. 2237 and No. 83, and Senate Report No. 93-983. One scholar has stated that these reports "will be weighed heavily in future court decisions on fair use," and there seems scant reason to doubt her appraisal. The documents reiterate the guidelines regarding fair use that are found in the Register's Report of 1961, although Senate Report No. 93-983 is the more recent and cogent of the three. All the Reports make it clear that photocopying by educators and librarians is to be governed by judicial interpretations of fair use. Senate Report No. 93-983 states that fair use in intendedin part to protect teachers who photocopy copyrighted works for classroom use and who are doing so in good faith. Section 107 of the present Copyright Revision Bill makes "it clear that . . . fair use can extend to the reproduction of copyrighted material for classroom teaching."

The views of copyright users, particularly of educators, toward the doctrine of fair use occasionally seem ambiguous. Over the years, users have uttered sentiments that betray both love and hate for the concept. Harry N. Rosenfield, counsel for educators in the copyright dispute, has at once spoken of its "wholly inadequate helpfulness" and also has referred to the doctrine as "a constant and continuing right." Nevertheless, it is clear that user interests deeply desire a statutory provision on fair use that incontrovertibly protects limited educational and scholarly copying and, in fact, gave up the traditional wording of the not-for-profit principle in exchange for just such a provision in the current Copyright Revision Bill as part of a political deal in 1966.

In summary, while fair use remains an elusive concept, it seems destined for statutory inclusion in a copyright revision bill as a protection against infringement suits for education, scholarly, and informational uses of copyrighted works. The four criteria used in determining its applicability in particular infringement cases will be subject to further refinement and relative balance by the courts. Nevertheless, fair use stands as additional official testimony that copyright is not inevitably the maximal means of creating and disseminating information.

The public domain policy, the not-for-profit limitation, and the fair use doctrine (including the notions of public and private use), amount to officially sanctioned statements of some significance which question the validity of copyright in terms of the public interest.

The public domain policy is of greatest concern to the executive branch of government, the not-for-profit principle is centered in the legislative branch, and the fair use doctrine is the contribution of the judicial branch. Copyright affects all branches of government, and all branches of government have taken substantial exeption to it as an adequate policy for knowledge management. Of such significance, in fact, are these three exceptions that a consideration of modifications and alternatives to copyright seems in order.

TRADITIONAL COPYRIGHT: PROPOSED MODIFICATIONS AND ALTERNATIVES

Policy Adaptations for a Technological Society

Before we plunge into a review of alternative policies to copyright that relfect the direct impact of the new information technologies, perhaps it would be appropriate to consider those options that, while not directly reflective of the influence of the new information technologies, have a growing appeal because of the more general conditions prevailing in a fast-changing technological society. Two proposals that deserve serious contemplation in this regard are the reduction of the copyright duration period and the institution of nonexclusive licenses to publish.

A copyright duration of the present potential fifty-six years appears somewhat excessive. It obstructs the republishing of information even when the original owner no longer publishes it (or never published it), and it can give exclusive control of knowledge to copyright owners for more than half a century. One recalls General Dodge's thinking on the usefulness of copyright as a censorship tool in this regard. If a person or institution can sit on sensitive information for fifty-six years, and even bring a likely successful court action against anyone who tries to disseminate that knowledge, then the information would be effectively censored. In this light it is noteworthy that the Soviet Union regards copyright as a most effective censor. The Soviets set up a new Copyright Agency as a result of Moscow's signing the International Copyright Convention in 1973. Boris D. Pankin, head to the agency, has stated that all Russian works to be published abroad first must go through his office. Should a Russian author circumvent the Copyright Agency, he would be subject to prosecution. Western observers have charged that Pankin's agency will be used to keep political dissidents from publishing abroad.

To contend that copyright is a potential ally of censorship is to consider only an extremity of the argument against excessive duration periods. But copyright indubitably can be a hindrance to the optimal dissemination of knowledge, and the longer that copyright applies to a work, the longer that information's distribution can be discouraged. Indeed, the initial five extensions of the Copyright Act of 1909 had, as 1971, kept about 70,000 volumes out of the public domain.

The voices being heard today argue that a long copyright duration not only should be retained but extended, from the current fifty-six years possible to the author's lifetime plus another half-century. The reasoning here is that the widows, widowers, and children of authors may be supported. Yet few, very few, authors take advantage of the present law as a means of supporting their spouses and progeny after their deaths. Barbara Ringer, the Register of Copyrights, has observed that only 15 percent of all copyrights are renewed. In other words, 85 percent of all copyright owners are quite content to make do with a copyright lasting twenty-eight years rather than the fifty-six that are available to them. In sum, the trend toward long periods of copyright duration seems increasingly dysfunctional as a public policy for knowledge management.

Exclusivity of licensing is the other major modification and the chief cause of monopolistic overtones in the copyright industry. By granting an exclusive license to a publisher to disseminate his work, an author permits that publisher to decide how much he should be paid for his effort. The publisher need not concern himself that a competitor will offer his author more remuneration because the law grants him an exclusive license to publish the work for fifty-six years, once the author signs the contract.

A nonexclusive license to publish would be more beneficial to authors than the present arrangement. Although it is possible that the excessive market power possessed by some book publishers has resulted in more profits for their authors by restricting entry into publishing, it seems probable that competition among publishers for valuable works would generally increase authors' revenues and book circulation as well. This could be accomplished by allowing authors to sign with a second publisher, provided that the second publisher reimburse the initial publisher for make-ready costs not yet recouped. Or, an initial publisher might be granted an exclusive license for a short period of time designed to reduce his financial risk, after which the author could let out his work for new bids. Nonexclusive licensing is a modification of copyright that offers some potentiality for increasing the income of authors while facilitating the dissemination of knowledge. In this regard, it offers a viable counter argument to those who urge lengthier periods of copyright duration as a means of enhancing the financial security of authors.

Policy Adaptations for the New Information Technologies

A shorter copyright duration and nonexclusive publishing licenses are two possible policy modifications that address the role of knowledge in a technological culture. Other proposals for modifying (or eliminating) copyright have, as their focal point of concern, the direct challenge posed to the creators and subsidizers of knowledge by the new information technologies.

A number of persons interested in the dissemination and control of knowledge have proposed multiple concepts of copyright, with each concept tailored to the particular medium to which it is applied. John Stedman of the American Association of University Professors and Attorney Charles H. Lieb have argued that "it will not be helpful to lump all kinds of publishing into one indistinguishable mass and to treat them alike." Bella L. Linden has suggested "the possible need for two laws, one a traditional copyright law for individual authors, and 'another to cover kinds of information, kinds of distribution and manipulation, and kinds of storage.' "

The notion of copyright laws tailored to media appears to be a legal echo of McLuhanesque perceptions of communications. Marshall McLuhan has made a case that no message is precisely transferrable from one medium to another and that, in a very real sense, the medium creates a new message and new conditions for the originator and recipient of the message. Thus, not only is the medium the message, but the experience, the "massage" of the artist and the public.

The idea of tailored copyrights has not yet been thought through. Nevertheless, tentative suggestions generally view photocopying and information storage and retrieval systems as concepts that theoretically can be administered under a single principle of knowledge management. Statutory fair use appears to be the most likely de facto (if not de jure) copyright law for neopublishing technologies, which currently has any chance for actual inclusion in the U.S. code. Abe A. Goldman of the Copyright Office has stated that "perhaps the extent of permissible reproduction by the computer will involve the same sort of fair use considerations as are presently to be seen in the problem of photocopying." Ralph S. Brown, Jr., of the Yale Law School, has noted that "Practically, ephemeral projections from photocopies and from computers should be treated alike, with considerable scope for fair use, and a library privilege of display to readers if the work displayed is legitimately in the possession of the library." Paul G. Zurkowski of the Information Industry Association has suggested "format copyright," statutory encouragement of licensing for reformatting data, and an identification numbering system for books as "post-Gutenberg copyright concepts." These updated versions of copyright would co-exist in tandem with traditional copyright, which Zurkowski believes to be more author- than publisher- or neopublisher-oriented.

Alternatives to copyright also have been forwarded. In law Professor Julius J. Marke's opinion, alternative means of compensating authors will develop naturally because "technological breakthrough will change the concept of author protection." He foresees authors selling their wares directly to information-system operators, with remuneration "based on use rather than on sales." Marke envisions a system in which scholarly works would be programmed into a highly sophisticated, national information network that tallied use units and compensated authors through prearranged accounting procedures. He concludes his scenario by positing users as subscribers to information networks (primarily students, teachers, and researchers), with dues to the system paid via a library fee.

The Ad Hoc Task Group on Legal Aspects Involved in National Information Systems of the Committee on Scientific and Technical Information, Federal Council for Science and Technology, also has addressed specifically the peculiarities of computers and copyright, and has identified some twenty proposals, ranging from the abolition of copyright to the elimination of all exemptions from copyright. These modifications and alternatives are worth some examination.

One group of these proposals emphasizes access to information by users as its prime value. These suggestions include the discarding in toto of the copyright concept; complete exemptions from copyright for information systems and institutions supporting federal programs, because they are "helping promote progress"; the establishment of a not-for-profit exemption; and exemptions for certain types of material, e.g., scientific and technical writings. The difficulty here is how to define such material. A final proposal which stresses access is that of exemptions for certain kinds of uses. This is a somewhat superior suggestion than that which urges particular types of material be exempted, but, in the opinion of the Ad Hoc Task Group, it shares the disadvantage of the second and third proposals, in that they could place inequitable burdens on nonexempted groups.

Other alternatives attempt to address the problems of compensation to the owners as well as access by the user. Included under this category is that of establishing broad exemptions with arrangements made for compensation. For example, lump sums could be paid to authors of technical materials. The reasoning here is that since three-quarters of all scientific and technical works are supported by the federal government, the government should pay for them. Or.

periodic payments could be made to authors and publishers for unrestricted use of updated tapes in information systems. Finally, recognition of the author could be granted by requiring reference to him when a certain number of his words are reproduced; this is in itself a form of compensation.

Other proposals trying to reconcile access with compensation deal with the institution of assessment periods. For instance, the granting of a moratorium on copyright infringement suits by nonprofit institutions during which time a study could be undertaken of the implications of computers for copyright law. Or, a study now, legislate later policy could be charted. Such a course, however, would place nonprofit groups under constraints that could be avoided by establishment of a moratorium. Finally, we could legislate now, but establish provisions in the law for a moratorium on inputs into information systems and a study of their copyright implications. Such a policy, unfortunately, could inhibit the free development of information storage and retrieval systems in the view of the Ad Hoc Task Group.

A final cache of proposals which attempts to balance access against compensation addresses licensing arrangements. For example, the institution of statutory licenses and fees for scientific, technical, and educational materials and users identified with these fields could be inaugurated. Under this proposal, operators of information storage and retrieval systems would make "a reasonable effort" to contact copyright owners, but could use their works whether contact was established or not. Payment (no fines, only normal royalties) would begin when, and if, the proprietors were found. Problems here revolve around defining scientific, technical, and educational materials to be licensed, defining uses and users of such materials, and the setting of fees. A similar suggestion urges the mandating of compulsory licensing and compulsory arbitration between copyright users and owners, i.e., bilateral negotiations that would result in private agreements. Finally, and reflecting a similar proposal made with photocopiers in mind is the institution of a copyright clearinghouse, through which users could buy "whole batches of information at once." Difficulties involved in a clearinghouse include the possibility that some owners might decide not to join, and antitrust problems over the control of clearinghouse sales of copyright licenses.

The third major thrust of suggestions dealing with copyright and the computer as identified by the Ad Hoc Task Group emphasizes compensation over access. One such proposal is legislate now, study later. The Ad Hoc Task Group prefers a moratorium to this option, as uninformed legislation could freeze nascent information systems into untoward patterns. Other alternative proposals for compensation are based on the setting up of bilateral negotiations between copyright users and owners, or the institution of contractual royalties or setting established standardized fees and requirements, using a computerized accounting system. Finally, there is the establishment of exclusive rights for the copyright owners with no exemptions granted. This is the opposite end of the spectrum from the first proposal, and equally fallacious in the opinion of the Ad Hoc Task Group.

Of these proposals, the Ad Hoc Task Group favors the granting of a moratorium on copyright infringement for nonprofit users during a study of computers and copyright. Its members believe that such a moratorium constitutes the most rational basis for arriving at some understanding of an ill-understood subject.

Other observers have focussed their suggestions on marketing options that could reduce or obviate the need for copyright. Law Professor Stephen Breyer is one of these commentators. Breyer states that "the case for copyright in the book trade is not a strong one generally and is even weaker for some parts of that trade." Nevertheless, Breyer concedes that, in the absence of copyright, other means might be deemed necessary to assure compensation for "an initial publisher of, say, a text with a long time horizon and large initial expenses," although he is not at all certain that even this kind of hypothetical situation would require a formal means for sustaining the book publisher's revenue. In any event, Breyer suggests that buyers, "individually or in groups, might contract to buy the book in advance of publication," before copying is possible. Or, alternatively, government subsidies could assure high-cost ventures by book publishers. Of these, Breyer favors the former. The facts that twenty-three states already adopt elementary textbooks at the state level, and that eighteen states adopt high school texts in the same fashion, indicate that book purchasers could organize without too much difficulty. Conversely, government subsidies always entail the risk of censored information.

Federally subsidized and disseminated information and the corresponding censorship risk are worth further examination. The developing reliance on the page charge by publishers of scientific and technical journals would appear to indicate that at least one system of disseminating information, without copyright and through federal subsidies, not only has evolved but has confronted the problems of government censorship as well. The page charge is a fee paid by research sponsors to journal publishers, usually on the basis of how many pages are required to print the research. Its purpose is to aid in information distribution by covering publication costs. The practice began overtly in 1930, when the American Physical Society authorized the editors of The Physical Review to charge institutions sponsoring research that they printed $2 a page to cover costs. Today, page charges range from 10 to 70 dollars, and a 1966 survey of 362 journals sponsored by the National Science Foundation showed that seventy-six of them levied page charges, while seventeen more billed for "excess" pages.

It was indicated earlier in this volume that few scientific journals rely on subscriptions as a major source of income. The major (and rising) source of income is the page charge. A 1966 survey by the Council of Biology Editors determined that page charges offset from 25 to 100 percent of the publication costs incurred by the journals they printed. In 1961, page charges met an average of nearly 36 percent of total publication costs for ten journals published by the American Institute of Physics, but in 1971 it was stated that about 80 percent of the publishing costs in physics are absorbed by the page charge.

The subscription price remains the other major source of journal income, and there is a direct relationship between it and the page charge. Science journal editors who have experimented with reducing or eliminating page charges have found it necessary to raise subscription rates unless they also derive considerable revenues from advertising. Higher subscription prices have not served to increase the circulation of information.

When a journal requests a page charge, it usually is the federal government that receives the bill. Page charges are a standard budgetary item in federal grant requests by scientists. Pressure for government-provided page charges began as early as 1947, and a sampling of grant budgets in the National Institutes of Health for fiscal year 1970 revealed that approximately 85 percent of the grantees requested publication costs. Such expenditures account for roughly 1.5 percent of the total awards, or from four to $6 million in a budget of $400 million.

In 1961, the Federal Council for Science and Technology officially sanctioned the idea that research is incomplete until published, and established standards for the budgeting and payment of page charges by federal agencies, research grantees, and government contractors. These standards are followed today, and have been adopted throughout the federal bureaucracy. More recently, the question has been raised as to whether a ceiling should be placed on page charges billed to the government. The 1966 National Science Foundation study, conducted by the Biological Communications Project of George Washington University, detected considerable variation in assessment of composition and make-ready costs, and urged that guidelines be set relating level of page charge to production costs. In 1970, a Task Group on the

Economics of Primary Publication of the Committee on Scientific and Technical Communication, National Academy of Sciences, called for a more extensive system of annually updating pertinent page charge information and recommended using the National Science Foundation's Office of Science Information as a monitoring agency.

Whether or not these proposed modifications of page charge practices are adopted, the current, operative system of federally supported journal publication has the advantage of avoiding both overtones of censorship and copyright restrictions. No central burea oversees page charges, and thus cannot favor particular journals. Yet, privately operated journals are receiving substantial federal subsidies.

Most of the preceding modifications and alternatives to the traditional copyright principle imply a reduction of its applicability to new informational forms. One suggestion, however, that seems worth further exploration advocates an extension of copyright's applicability. Robert P. Henderson, Vice-President of Honeywell Information Systems, recently urged the Senate Subcommittee on Constitutional Rights to make "personal information" a "property right." Such a definition would permit citizens access to all data banks and dossiers, in order to "determine for themselves when, how, and what information is communicated to others." Citizens would have recourse to the courts in the event they disagreed with how their personal information was used.

Henderson's view amounts to a novel interpretation of copyright, but one that is in tune with current informational problems of American society. Henderson is saying that what a citizen <u>does</u> is "copyrightable" by the citizen who does it, but those who compile records of what that citizen does should not have their works protected by copyright. Because the citizen has copyrighted, in effect, his behavior, he may disseminate records of his behavior as he sees fit.

It is not the point of this Chapter to advocate some new system for encouraging information production and its dissemination, but rather to suggest that modifications of and alternatives to copyright are practical and very likely worthwhile in a knowledgeable society. It is up to politicians to decide which modifications are most practical, and it is up to academicians to decide which alternatives are most worthwhile.

REFERENCES

American Council on Education (1963). Staff memoranda prepared in connection with the study on copyrights, clearances and rights of teachers in the new educational media. Prepared under the

Direction of Fred S. Siebert, Dean, College of Communication Arts, Michigan State University, East Lansing, Michigan. Washington: American Council on Education.

American Society of Composers Authors and Publishers (1970). Copyright Law Symposium: Number Eighteen. Nathan Burkan Memorial Competition. New York: Columbia University Press.

Biological Sciences Communication Project of the George Washington University (1968). Scientific journal page charge practice. A report prepared for the National Science Foundation. Washington: U.S. Government Printing Office.

Breyer, Stephen (1970). The uneasy case for copyright: A study of copyright in books, photocopies, and computer programs. Harvard Law Review LXXXIV, December, 281-351.

Brown, Ralph S., Jr. (1969). Appendix: Copyright problems of research libraries. In On research libraries. Statement and recommendations of the Committee on Research Libraries of the American Council of Learned Societies. Submitted to the National Advisory Commission on Research Libraries, November, 1967. Cambridge, Massachusetts: The M.I.T. Press, 86-100.

Brucker, Herbert (1967). Profits from public papers: The government copyright racket. Saturday Review, August 11, 1962. Reprinted in U.S. Congress, Senate, Committee on the Judiciary, Subcommittee on Patents, Trademarks, and Copyrights, Copyright Law Revision, Hearings before Subcommittee on Patents, Trademarks, and Copyrights. Pursuant to S. Res. 37 on S. 597, Part 2, 90th Cong., 1st Sess., March 20, 21, and April 4, 1967. Washington: U.S. Government Printing Office, 651-654.

Bugbee, Bruce W. (1967). Genesis of American patent and copyright law. Washington: Public Affairs Press.

Bush, George P. (Ed.) (1972). Technology and copyright: An annotated bibliography and source materials. Mt. Airy, Maryland: Lomond Systems, Inc.

A call for legislation to make personal information a property right (1971). EDP Weekly XI, March 8, 1-2.

Cambridge Research Institute (1973). Omnibus copyright revision: Comparative analysis of the issues, Arthur B. Hanson (Ed.). Washington: American Society for Information Science.

Collins, Carole and Schick, Frank L. (Eds). The Bowker annual of library and book trade information, 1970. New York: R. R. Bowker, p. 582, 8.

Federal Council for Science and Technology (1967). Committee on Scientific and Technical Information. Ad Hoc Task Group on Legal Aspects Involved in National Information Systems. The copyright law as it relates to national information systems and national programs. A study by the Ad Hoc Task Group on Legal Aspects Involved in National Information Systems, PB-175 618, July, 1967. Washington: U.S. Government Printing Office.

Goldman, Abe A. (1971). Copyright as it affects libraries: Legal implications. In Encyclopedia of library and information science (Volume 6), Allen Kent and Harold Lancour (Eds.). New York: Marcel Dekker, Inc., pp. 63-75.

Goldman, Abe A. (1964). The concept of the law of copyright. In Reprography and copyright law, Lowell H. Hattery and George P. Bush (Eds.). Baltimore, Maryland: Port City Press, Inc., 11-17.

Kaplan, Benjamin and Miller, Arthur R. (1967). Computers and the copyright bill. EDUCOM: Bulletin of the Interuniversity Communications Council II, April, 3-6, 8-11.

Kestenbaum, Lionel (1970). The regulatory context of information utilities. Varieties in law and public policy. In The information utility and social choice, Harold Sackman and Norman Nie (Eds.). Montvale, New Jersey: AFIPS Press, 73-101.

Latman, Alan (1960). Study no. 14: Fair use of copyrighted works. March, 1958. In Copyright law revision. Studies prepared for the Subcommittee on Patents, Trademarks, and Copyrights of the Committee on the Judiciary, U.S. Senate. 86th Cong., 2nd Sess. Pursuant to S. Res. 250, studies 14-16. Washington, U.S. Government Printing Office, 1-44.

Lazowska, Mrs. Edward S. (1968). Photocopying, copyright, and the librarian. American Documentation XIX, April, 123-130.

Legality of governmental copyrighting challenged by leading editors and scholars (1967). Reprinted in U.S. Congress, Senate, Committee on the Judiciary, Subcommittee on Patents, Trademarks, and Copyrights. In Copyright law revision. Hearing before Subcommittee on Patents, Trademarks, and Copyrights. Pursuant to S. Res. 37 on S. 597, Part 2, 90th Cong., 1st Sess., March 20, 21, and April 4, 1967. Washington: U.S. Government Printing Office, 650-651.

Long, Russell B. (1967). Statement before the Education Subcommittee, Labor and Public Welfare Committee, U.S. Senate. Reprinted in U.S. Congress, Senate, Committee on the Judiciary,

Subcommittee on Patents, Trademarks, and Copyrights. In Copyright law revision. Hearings before . . . Pursuant to S. Res. 37 on S. 597, Part 2, 90th Cong., 1st Sess., March 20, 21, and April, 1967. Washington: U.S. Government Printing Office, 655-658.

Marke, Julius J. (1967). Copyright and intellectual property. New York: The Fund for the Advancement of Education.

Mylecraine, Walter E. (1967). Public domain. American Education. November, 1965. Reprinted in U.S. Congress, Senate, Committee on the Judiciary, Subcommittee on Patents, Trademarks, and Copyrights. In Copyright law revision. Hearings before . . . Puruant to S. Res. 37 on S. 597, Part 2, 90th Cong., 1st Sess., March 20, 21, and April 4, 1967. Washington: U.S. Government Printing Office, 658-651.

Nicholson, Margaret (1970). A manual of copyright practice for writers, publishers, and agents. New York: Oxford University Press, XIV, 273.

Organization for Economic and Cultural Development (1968). Reviews of national science policy: United States. Paris: OECD.

Patterson, Lyman Ray (1971). Copyright and the public interest. In Encyclopedia of library and information science (Volume 6), Allen Kent and Harold Lancour (Eds.). New York: Marcel Dekker, Inc., 76-82.

Pforzheimer, Walter L. (1964). Historical perspective on copyright law and fair use. In Reprography and copyright law, Lowell H. Hattery and George P. Bush (Eds.). Baltimore, Maryland: Port City Press, Inc., 18-35.

Pilpel, Harriet F. and Zavin, Theodora S. (1969). Rights and writers: A handbook of literary and entertainment law. New York: E. P. Dutton and Co., Inc.

Roberts, Matt (1970). Copyright: A selected bibliography of periodical literature relating to literary property in the United States. Metuchen, N.J.: Scarecrow Press.

Rosenfield, Harry N. (1968). Major problems of copyright law as viewed by the Ad Hoc Committee on Copyright Law Revision (mimeo). Washington: Ad Hoc Committee of Educational Institutions and Organizations on Copyright Law Revision, p. 62.

Rosenfield, Harry N. (1967). Statement. In Copyright law revision. Hearings before the Subcommittee on Patents, Trademarks, and Copyrights of the Committee on the Judiciary, U.S. Senate, 90th Cong., 1st Sess. Pursuant to S. Res. 37 on S. 597, Part 4, April 28, 1967. Washington: U.S. Government Printing Office, 1063-1065.

Scal, Marjorie (1971). The page charge. Scholarly Publishing III, October, 62-69.

Schnapper, M. B. (1960). Constraint by copyright: A report on "official" and "private" practices. Washington: Public Affairs Press.

Schnapper, M. B. (1967). Statement. U.S. Congress, Senate, Committee on the Judiciary, Subcommittee on Patents, Trademarks, and Copyrights. In Copyright Law Revision, Hearings before Subcommittee on Patents, Trademarks, and Copyrights. Pursuant to S. Res. 37 on S. 597, Part 2, 90th Cong., 1st Sess., March 21, 1967. Washington: U.S. Government Printing Office, 646-650.

Shaw, Ralph R. (1964). Copyright in relation to copying of scholarly materials. In Reprography and copyright law, Lowell H. Hattery and George P. Bush (Eds.). Baltimore, Maryland: Port City Press, Inc., 93-98.

Siebert, Fred S. (1964). Copyrights, clearances, and rights of teachers in the new educational media. Report of a study by Fred S. Siebert. Made for the Commission on Academic Affairs of the American Council on Education under a grant from the Office of Education, U.S. Department of Health, Education, and Welfare. Washington: American Council on Education, V, p. 62.

Smith, Robert H. (1968). USOE issues its copyright guidelines. Publishers' Weekly CXCIV, August 12, p. 36.

Task Group on the Economics of Primary Publication (1970). Committee on Scientific and Technical Communication. National Academy of Sciences — National Academy of Engineering. Report of the Task Group on the Economics of Primary Publication. Washington: National Academy of Sciences.

Varmer, Borge (1960). Study no. 15: Photoduplication of copyrighted material libraries. May, 1959. In Copyright Law Revision. Studies prepared for the Subcommittee on Patents, Trademarks, and Copyrights of the Committee on the Judiciary, United States Senate, 86th Cong., 2nd Sess. Pursuant to S. Res. 240. Studies 14-16. Washington: U.S. Government Printing Office, 45-67.

White, Leonard D. (1959). The federalists: A study in administrative history. New York: The Macmillan Company.

Zurkowski, Paul G. (1968-1969). Post-Gutenberg copyright concepts. NMA Journal II, Winter, 70-73.

U.S. Congress (1961). House. Committee on the Judiciary. Copyright law revision. Part 1. Report of the Register of Copyrights on the General Revision of the U.S. Copyright Law, 87th Cong., 1st Sess. July, 1961. Washington: U.S. Government Printing Office.

U.S. Congress (1966). House. Committee on the Judiciary. Copyright law revision. Report No. 2237 to accompany H.R. 4347, 89th Cong., 2nd Sess. October 12, 1966. Washington: U.S. Government Printing Office.

U.S. Congress (1967). House. Committee on the Judiciary. Copyright law revision. Report No. 83 to accompany H.R. 2512, 90th Cong., 1st Sess. March 8, 1967. Washington: U.S. Government Printing Office.

U.S. Congress (1974). Senate. Committee on the Judiciary. Copyright law revision. Report No. 93-983 together with Additional and Minority Views. To accompany S. 1361. Calendar No. 946, July 3, 1974, 93rd Cong., 2nd Sess. Washington: U.S. Government Printing Office.

U.S. Congress (1969). House. Committee on the Judiciary. Copyright protection in certain cases. Report No. 91-641 to accompany S. J. Res. 143, 91st Cong., 1st Sess. November 18, 1969. Washington: U.S. Government Printing Office.

U.S. Congress (1973). Senate. Committee on the Judiciary. Subcommittee on Patents, Trademarks, and Copyrights. Copyright law revision. Hearings before Subcommittee on Patents, Trademarks, and Copyrights, 93rd Cong., 1st Sess. Pursuant to S. Res. 56 on S. 1361, July 31 and August 1, 1973. Washington: U.S. Government Printing Office.

Chapter 5

THE FUTURE AS INFORMATION

After considering some options to copyright as a public policy for knowledge management, it is but a short step to speculation on the future role of knowledge in technological cultures. Sober men have argued that society is no more than its communications, that information is all. Recently, this argument appears to have increased its persuasive powers in a variety of social, scholarly, scientific, and political circles. Suddenly we are bombarded with such concepts as "noosphere," "noetic authority," "knowledgeable society," "new utopians," "politics of expertise," "invisible college," "technocracy," "postcivilization," and "the medium is the massage," to list only a few. These phrases. which among other contentions, express the beliefs that information will assume a dominant economic and social role in a society, and that new patterns of knowledge usage will engender a new kind of politics, have assumed a revitalized credibility in an age characterized by an information explosion and mysterious information technologies.

It is my purpose in this concluding chapter to examine a few of the implications of information and information technologies for American social dynamics of the future. And so doing, I shall review some possibilities concerning the impact of the new information technologies on certain information-sensitive and copyright-oriented professions, the democratic political process, and man's image of himself. In reading this discussion, one might keep in mind the scenario on the future development of the new information technologies that we posited in Chapter 2: The new technologies are homogenizing and becoming extremely pervasive in their cultural impact.

IMPLICATIONS OF INFORMATION TECHNOLOGY FOR THE INFORMATION PROFESSIONS

Profound changes for information-related professions (notably authors, publishers, academics, researchers, educators, and copyright bureaucrats) stemming from technology are appearing on the horizon. For example, the bureaucratization of authors seems increasingly plausible. Authors long have been loners, and the popular image of the author is that of a Joycean figure scribbling in the recesses of an underheated garrett. In fact, however, this life style of writers has been waning for some time.

Science provides a case in point. Creativity in science was a highly individualistic process until World War II. Geometry, calculus, gravity, electricity, and the germ theory were discoveries made by individual scientists working on their own. With the Naxi threat, Big Science, organized, team-oriented science, suddenly emerged. While individual genius is still vital, the milieu in which scientific genius now functions is radically different from that of forty years ago. Grantsmanship, R & D management, the scientific estate, and the National Science Foundation, among other facts of laboratory life in the 1970s were unknown in 1930.

As science has been bureaucratized, so might be intellectual creativity in general. The professionalization of the professoriate from the late 1800s through the early 1900s in this country (e.g., the rise of professional associations of scholars and the recognition of the Ph.D. as an advanced teaching certificate) already has accomplished in part the bureaucratization of writing.

The explosion of data technologies should encourage the bureaucratization process considerably more. As computers become increasingly responsible for the dissemination of information, it seems likely that information system operators will avoid the publishing middle man and contract directly with authors to prepare works specifically for computers. Many of these kinds of writings probably will be developed through team efforts, just as many computer programs are now. This should change the author's psychological identification with his work and, conceivably, his psychic relationship with society. In some instances, computers themselves will become authors, in that they can be programmed in a manner so sophisticated as to legitimately claim authorship of original works.

Should policymakers, because of growing neopublishing practices, decide to abandon the copyright concept as society's chief method of rewarding intellectual effort, it also seems probable that a more bureaucratic means of reimbursement will be substituted. In the Soviet Union, for example, this already has occurred, an author is paid according to the number of copies of his work that the State decides to print. Censorship problems, inherent in Russian information policies, are not an inevitable aspect of all information policies that reject the copyright concept. Nevertheless, the bureaucratization of authorship does seem to be a near-inevitability. Authors may find themselves on a payroll.

Publishers stand the most to lose from new information technologies. With every man and his Xerox machine his own publisher, traditional publishing houses appear increasingly like the dinosaur. Our tentative scenario in this book gives no room for the relief of private publishers; as information networks develop, shelves of books in the home will become more decorative than utilitarian.

A variety of observers have urged publishers to go electronic, and have predicted their demise unless they do. The implication of such predictions in that publishing houses will continue to dominate the information marketplace by diversification and merger. A secondary implication is that the numerous publishing houses now dotting the country (about 900) will remain numerous, if in a slightly more electronic form.

An opposite prediction seems more compatible with current facts, that electronic information companies, as exemplified by Xerox Corporation, will absorb publishing houses. This forecast implies that the information industry will not remain relatively diffused, as it is now, but will become increasingly oligopolistic. Not only are the managements and technologies of the information industry homogenizing, but they are homogenizing within quite limited corporate confines. By way of example, there are less than ten companies of any consequence in the United States that manufacture high-speed digital computers.

Should the great bulk of data dissemination capacities come under the control of a small group of electronic industrial giants, new problems of knowledge management are likely to arise. It is conceivable, for example, that antibusiness values will be less represented than they are now in the information spectrum.

Finally, as electronic information firms absorb publishing houses, the life style of the traditional publisher may alter; the tweedy, horn-rimmed stereotype of the book publisher may be replaced by the equally stereotyped management team of IBM, uniform in white shirts and black plastic glasses. As a business, publishing is relatively unstructured. With the advent of electronic data dissemination, this should change.

Other information professionals may be affected even more profoundly by new information technologies. Librarians, for example, are extraordinarily image-conscious. A recent advertising campaign by American Motors, which excluded only librarians among those people who would be interested in a hot new model that the Company was unveiling, drew such an adverse response from librarians nationwide that American Motors bought full-page advertisements in major library journals, apologizing for the faux pas. Librarians are not at all happy with their professional image of a wizened old lady who hisses "Quiet, please!" at patrons.

Information technology may change not only the image but the reality of librarians. As information networks develop, the camera and screwdriver may replace the card catalog and rubber stamp as the librarian's tools. Librarians seem amenable to this development; they want to be "groovy," and the sophisticated world of information technology permits this eventuality more readily than stacks of books that need dusting.

Librarians are concerned principally with the interests of researchers, another group of knowledge professionals. The "publish or perish" diktat in universities has fostered a publication competition among researchers that has added immeasurably to the data explosion. While technology offers a means of controlling this explosion, information technology and academic realities concerning publication should combine to accelerate the life style of the professoriate. Technology greatly factilitates research, making it possible for professors to publish more and faster. This, in turn, intensifies the publication competition on the campus, ultimately increasing the publication inflation.

Faster research abilities via technology, and therefore more research findings, could cancel each other out. Researchers would be publishing more and more rapidly, but the enormity of raw data produced would be growing as well. In terms of learning and knowledge, of generating information that can be controlled, comprehended, managed, and used for social purposes, society would be back where it started. The only differences would be of size and speed: more research, more data, more technology, and much faster life styles in academe.

Of course, a more optimistic view, and perhaps a more likely eventuality, is possible, that data technology actually will enable scholars, scientists, policymakers, and other citizens to control the data explosion. Should this occur, we shall, in theory at least, have a better chance of understanding our society and ourselves.

Perhaps more than any other single participant in the information professions, new data technologies will affect educators. And, as information technology alters education, so will it alter us all.

The Council on Library Resources, the Interuniversity Communications Council, and computer scientist Anthony G. Oettinger have been instrumental in developing what Juergen Schmandt of Harvard's Program on Technology and Society aptly calls, "the Vision." The Vision refers to the vast information network hypothesized in our scenario, but with an educational emphasis. The Vision posits a new breed of teacher, who must know more about people than the three R's; machinery will allow teachers to be more humanistic than mechanical. Machines will take over and improve the simple transmission-of-culture aspect of teaching, giving the teacher greater opportunity to concentrate on the pupil's emotional development. Guidance becomes to all-important.

Even more significantly, the Vision implies that learning will become a life-long experience, ultimately centered in the home. School is never out, it is forever. Conceivably, every child could have access to a home information terminal that would teach him letters and numbers through a series of "Sesame Street"-like programs. After that, in theory, toddlers (or their parents) could educate themselves through an elective system similar to that prevalent in universities today, possibly modeled after the Open University currently operating in England.

Paul Armer, Director of the Stanford University Computation Center, has calculated that a national continuing education program, "somewhat in the nature of the social security system" and relying heavily on information technology, would cost about $8,000 per person involved annually. With 5 percent of a labor force of roughly 70 million in continuing education, there would be an approximate yearly cost of $30 billion, or about 3 percent of our Gross National Product. By comparison, our defense establishment spends about 6 percent of our GNP per year. Eventually, the costs of an education-oriented information utility could be more than offset by an expected increase in productivity.

Despite great economic potential, however, a problem with the Vision is that it assumes teachers will be just as needed in nonhuman-based instructional systems as they are now, but for more noble reasons, the socialization and molding of children rather than the mundane transmission of culture. There is no factual basis for believing this. Futurist Herman Kahn has argued, from empirical evidence, that computer-based teaching machines do a far better job at developing security and a sense of self-esteem in children that do flesh-and-blood teachers with all their human foibles. In his words, nonhuman-based instruction "beats every teacher the kid has got, and the kids know it." Moreover, "there is a certain tendency for the children to get fixated on the computer," and he adds:

> People will pick a very warm nurture, a soft and gentle voice, a computer voice. When the kid goes in and spends an hour a day, the computer always says to him, "How are you, Johnny?" Never gets his name wrong. Very pleasant with him. Never loses its temper. Will repeat, over and over again, but always with a kind of fresh interest. It says, "Goodbye, Johnny," when he leaves.

A second problem with the Vision is its feasibility. Oettinger has scored the Vision not only in terms of mechanical practicality, but of political probability. He is especially critical of the American educational establishment as one designed to resist change. Education in the United States is bureaucratically rigid, organizationally fragmented, economically poor, and politically rich. When confronted with a Vision that threatens to displace teachers and even the school house itself, innovating to accomodate that Vision does not seem to be in education's hand of cards.

Conversely, Burton R. Clark has contended the opposite, that the chaotic system of American education is amenable to change, but that the need for coordination among its parts is maximized. He cites the case of new physics in U.S. secondary schools. University professors, secondary school teachers, businessmen, and the National Science Foundation coordinated their activities in such a way as to have more than 40 percent of the nation's high school students learning the new physics ten years after the program's initiation. In this incident, however, no one had anything to lose, save those teachers who could not adapt (but who probably did not have to adapt). This would not seem to be the case with the introduction to the classroom of education technology.

A final professional group that is likely to undergo considerable alteration as a result of new information technologies is the federal copyright bureaucracy. The copyright bureaucracy includes agencies throughout the federal establishment, particularly in the National Science Foundation, the Library of Congress, the Federal Communications Commission, and the Departments of Defense and Health, Education, and Welfare, but is centered in the U.S. Copyright Office. As the social impact of information technology intensifies, the Copyright Office's function of registration may wane in favor of regulation.

At first glance, the crass, political style of a regulatory agency, à la Interstate Commerce Commission, hardly would seem applicable to the bookish image of copyright officials. The Copyright Office is a government bureau that often conjures images of green eye-shades and arm garters for the public-at-large. The anomaly of the "register" title itself seems quaint. A registrar denotes a person, while a register normally refers to a place, a book, or a machine. On being asked why the term "register" should be continued as the title of the director of the Copyright Office, Register Abraham L. Kaminstein replied that he rather favored its continuance because, "there are any number of registrars; there is only one Register."

The process of selecting the Register also is characterized by quaintness. Evidently, legislators originally perceived the Register's duties as more clerical than political, and none of the normal checks-and-balances is formally necessary in appointing a successor to the office. Thus, appointment of the Register of Copyrights is legally the sole decision of the Librarian of Congress.

The politicization of the Copyright Office has paralleled the growth of information technology. Until Arthur Fisher's appointment (Register of Copyrights from 1951 to 1960), only librarians and publishers had taken any interest in the post. While there was a slight increase in the number of groups expressing interest over Fisher's appointment, there were even more concerned parties in 1960 when Kaminstein took over. In 1971, raw, interest-group politics in the selection of a Register of Copyrights was apparent. Not only were authors, educators, electronics firms, librarians, congressmen, lawyers, publishers, and other groups evident in the selection process, but political issues such as due process of law, racial discrimination, and women's lib were very much present as well.

Arthur Miller, then of the University of Michigan Law School and a scholar of computers' ramifications for copyright and personal privacy, was widely reported as Librarian of Congress L. Quincy Mumford's first choice. Some sources said that he had actually been given the job. A number of groups, particularly librarians and members of the copyright bar, objected to Mumford's selection, while certain members of Congress feared that the effort to revise the copyright law would be disrupted by appointing an outside academic to the post. An additional factor, in the view of some observers, was simply that not enough groups had been consulted, and that the flurry arose more in objection to the political method rather than to the man.

With an outside man excluded, Mumford then picked an inside man for the job: George D. Cary, Deputy Register of Copyrights. Members of the copyright bar felt that, while Cary was the most qualified politically, he was "perhaps not the best qualified as a technician of copyright law," as Publishers' Weekly delicately phrased it. Immediately, Barbara A Ringer, Assistant Register of Copyrights, filed suit in U.S. District Court, requesting a restraining order on Cary's appointment on the ground that the U.S. Civil Service Commission had failed to observe its own regulations in making the appointment.

It later developed that Register Kaminstein had recommended Ringer as his successor to Mumford, and that Mumford apparently had agreed to his recommendation, at least until 1968. But Ringer, who is white, had represented dissident blacks during a racially tense situation in the Copyright Office that had culminated in 1970. In this light, Ringer also filed a complaint with the Library of Congress's Fair Employment Practices Office, alleging racial and sexual bias in Mumford's appointment of Cary. Although the U.S. District Court ruled that Mumford's appointment procedures had not followed Civil Service regulations, Cary had the title of Acting Register of Copyrights throughout the appellate proceedings. Finally, in late 1973, the two-year imbroglio culminated when a federal appellate court ordered that Cary vacate the Office of the Register on the grounds that he had been appointed partially on the basis of racial and sexual discrimination. Ringer is the current Register of Copyrights.

The events surrounding the appointment procedures of the "sensitive position" (as Publishers' Weekly called it) of the Register of Copyrights, indicate the newly politicized character of the post. Politics and regulation stroll hand-in-hand in America, and while politics does not necessarily lead to regulation, politics plus widespread neopublishing practices would seem to make the Copyright Office a prime candidate for regulatory responsibilities. Proposals for a copyright clearinghouse are designed to regulate the dissemination of information in society through administrative rather than market mechanisms, and likely would center on the Copyright Office.

There are a number of studies by political scientists on the behavior of regulatory agencies. Their conclusions are uniform, that regulatory agencies ultimately are captured by those interests they are meant to regulate.

Should the Copyright Office become a regulator of information disseminators might capture it. Librarians and educators already believe that the Copyright Office is pro-proprietor in its views on copyright revision (although there is little evidence to support their belief), simply because its officialdom is committed to the continuation of the copyright principle.

With the rapid development of information technology and potential concomitant changes in copyright arrangements, organizations other than publishing firms probably will be the information disseminators of the future, e.g., electronics companies, television networks, computer firms, microphotography corporations, and photocopier manufacturers. These businesses would have the keenest interest in the regulator policies of the federal copyright bureaucracy.

INFORMATION TECHNOLOGY AND POLITICS

Neopublishing practices have questioned in tangible form the private property concept in the United States. Now the copyright user also may be the copyright owner by virtue of his access to a photocopier or computer. Copyright is inextricably linked with the printing press, a costly machine that traditionally has been easy to control in terms of use once it has been purchased. With photocopiers, everyone produces copyrighted works for himself, and thus effectively owns the copyright. More significantly, because of photocopiers and other information machinery the state is powerless to protect that which it historically has been obligated to protect: private property, in this case, private intellectual property as identified by its copyrighted status.

This concrete demeaning of the sanctity of private property by new information technologies is in harmony with a larger movement on the American scene that favors communal collectivism over proprietary notions. Much of this movement rests on that newly discovered caste, youth. Charles Reich's "Consciousness III" and Theodore Roszak's counter culture provide cultural frameworks that posit a liberation of Western man from property, materialism, and power neuroses. Property, whether real, liquid, or intellectual, may be fading as a viable concept in the West.

Private property, its reality and its ideology, is a mainstay of the middle class. To detract from its political significance should reduce the power base of the middle class. The scenarios offered by Roszak and particularly by Reich may alter the political role of the middle class ultimately in the more profound sense. Nevertheless, the copyright industry, on which economic analysts place greater significance than banking, mining, and utilities in terms of impact on the economy, could be affected far more readily by information technology. Information technology also should dramatize the inability of the state to protect private property as currently defined, thus contributing to the alienation of the middle class from the polity.

More importantly, information technology has far greater potentiality for expanding the political significance of the middle class, rather than reducing it. The middle (and upper) class has both the inclination and the money to buy information services, which probably will be available only on a commercial basis initially. The middle class should dominate the commercial information utility in the short run, and this domination should exacerbate its relations with other socio-economic groups and non-WASP minorities.

But if there is danger in the middle class dominating information networks, in the sense of providing the attitudinal market for commercial network operators to the exclusion of other groups, there is even more danger that information networks ultimately could provide a highly usable means of manipulating not only the middle class but the whole of society as well. Data networks can be set up in such a way so that each citizen with an information terminal in his home can encode his information profile on the memory banks of a central computer. Stafford Beer, a specialist in cybernetics, has posited a straight-forward scenario in this regard. Assume there are twenty buttons on your television set, and that a trustworthy broadcaster like Walter Cronkite (or, if you prefer, Burt Parks) asks you to participate in a personal response program. You, the viewer, are shown two pictures and asked to press either a "like" or "dislike" button in response. This process is repeated twenty times. Then the announcer suggests that you press a "print" button. A highly profile-specific, "you-oriented" message then appears, either in printed or televised form, or both.

A central computer would be capable of distinguishing between more than 1 million different information profiles in such system, for there are 2^{20} ways in which the buttons can be pressed. And this is on the basis of only one program. With several programs, the information could be updated and recorded (legally or illegally) by respondent, thus building a vast cumulative file in an advertiser's or government's computer memory core.

Given the kinds of functions such information networks probably would be performing for the individual citizen (e.g., learning, banking, ordering groceries, and conceivably worshipping and voting electronically) and for the corporation and government (e.g., advertising, teaching, market researching, opinion polling, and conceivably direct surveillance and bugging), extremely detailed information on every citizen could be recorded and stored. Some of the more obvious kinds of information that would interest public or private investigators are: the respondent's medical history, marital status, credit rating, degree of formal education, bank balance, religious, political, and social views, employment status, family context, and his intimate psychological situation.

Once such data are gathered and stored in usable form, information derived from feedback that the individual citizen himself supplies willingly, then highly user-directed massages can be sent. The dangers of information network operators misusing this power already have been hinted: "irresistable" commercial and political appeals, each one tailored to the individual respondent and delivered to him electronically in his home. It is not inconceivable that televised broadcasters might be correlated to individual terminal users on the basis of personality compatibility, thus further enhancing the client appeal tailored by network operators. For example, a respondent with an authoritarian personality might find himself conversing electronically with an announcer whose ortatory style is reminiscent of Benito Mussolini. The image politics spawned in the 1960s is still at the pablum stage when we consider the prospects of information networks predicated on the feedback principle.

Of course, the potential benefits of information technology are at least equal in magnitude to its danger. Most notable in this regard is education. In a very real sense, with a fully developed information network the student becomes his own teacher; he chooses that which he is most inclined to learn, and at his own pace without dysfunctional competitive pressure. Not only is the student his own teacher, but his own editor, publisher, telecaster, researcher, and writer as well.

This is an ability that can be granted only by technology in a technological society. Yet, paradoxically, it is also a sought-for return to the medieval practice of custom-tailored publishing. As Beer notes, "We shall use the power of computers to undertake an editing process on behalf of the only editor who any longer counts — the client himself." More fundamentally, in a biological sense, custom-tailored editing connotes that data will be transmitted far more parsimoniously, in that data will be true information, i.e., knowledge that changes us. Organisms can absorb and use only a limited quantity of stimuli. Stimuli that the organism itself chooses to receive are more likely to be usable to that organism than are stimuli selected and edited by another.

This potential ability to be one's own editor and teacher may be subject to at least one qualification. The individual client at the home information terminal must choose what he wants to read, see, and hear according to descriptors that are codified by those controlling the information network. The responsibility for defining descriptors and determining what data bits are to be categorized under which descriptor yields a subtle but potent censoring power to the network controller. Information can be effectively hidden in the system, and those who hide it are extremely well protected from accounting for their actions. For example, should a network controller decide to categorize the hypothetical fact of excessive corporate profits in the tulip bulb industry under "soil science," or some equally bizarre descriptor, that fact would be censored by virtue of its unlikely discovery on the part of a future Ralph Nader. More broadly, network controllers could become the new politicians, with political skill defined as informational expertise rather than as electoral experience.

A related political facet of information networks is their implication for social decision making. Will such networks increase or diminish democratic participation in the public policy-making process?

Information theorist Donald N. Michael foresees computer-based planning as the central political variable in the policy-making process of the future, and recognizes that the computer factor could dehumanize the polity on a very fundamental scale. As an answer to the potential problem posed by the computer, he relies on a computer solution. Michael urges that information citizen terminals be scattered throughout cities, in order that out-groups can have access to the same data used by urban planners. Ethnic groups, the poor, and those most affected by planning could develop alternate plans and use their plans as a means of resistance against the designs of officials, as well as "look over the shoulder of the planner and decision-maker as they prepare their plans and decisions."

An even more optimistic view holds that, with the advent of information utilities, voters will participate more frequently and more directly, and that individualized citizen contacts with public policymakers will increase. While the notion of an electronic "town meeting of the air" or a "global village" has been discarded by several political scientists as too simplistic, the fact remains that voter registration procedures and requirements remain among the greatest obstacles to voting. A home-based information utility, in which everyone could register his opinion on issues with maximal convenience, probably would have substantial effects on voter participation. Also, if the information utility were rigged in such a way so that a citizen could discover what agency was responsible for what policy that affected him (e.g., social security or workman's compensation), particular grievances could be registered and handled much more quickly than they are presently, thus increasing the responsiveness of the polity to the plight of the individual citizen.

With individual citizens having genuine personal access to policymakers as a result of a pervasive information utility, we can foresee the debureaucratization of the lobbyist. Votes are the legislator's currency, and money is only an indirect way of buying votes via costly campaigns. With a directly participatory democracy enabled by information technology, the influence of organized interest groups, which is based on ready campaign contributions and carefully cultivated access to policymakers, could be undermined radically.

We also can expect the factionalization of interest groups as a result of the impact of the information utility. Because the costs of obtaining access to policymakers would be reduced by the information utility, interested citizens could coalesce around highly particularistic demands with considerable economy. Such an eventuality ultimately could have ramifications for the two-party system in this country.

There is a darker side to the politics of an information utility, however, and one that unfortunately seems to be a more plausible outcome: that information technology may increase the isolation of public policymakers from the populace. One dimension of this phenomenon can be seen from the perspective of the governed. After analyzing the television viewing habits of various social, educational, and economic strata in the United States, political scientist Norman Nie observed a positive correlation between long hours of home viewing and low rates of political participation. He concluded that "the differential impact of home viewing on the more interested and informed citizen could . . . reduce the overall quality of participation by leveling the differences of rates in political activity among those who vary in interest and information." Because of its high entertainment value (the average American much prefers to watch entertainment rather than public information programs on television), Nie adds, the information utility actually could decrease political participation and "may quite likely contribute to a privatization of social life." Such opinions recall the caveats of the ancient Greeks on the ignorant involvement in policymaking spawned by democracy.

Nie's thoughts on the privatization of citizens represent one side of the coin in terms of how public policymakers may be isolated increasingly from their publics by information technology. The other side of the coin refers to the policymakers themselves. We know more than you long has been a phrase used by politicos to justify controversial decisions. The war in Vietnam comes readily to mind. Control of information is the cornerstone of conventional politics. The justification of decisions, the presentation of issues, the evaluation of polls, and the construction of images are central to the retention of power. To undermine informational control is to change politics as we understand it. It seems likely, therefore, that policymakers will use data technology to enhance rather than reduce their control of information if they are at all able to do so.

Futurist Robert Boguslaw has offered a comprehensive explanation of how information technology can yield greater decision-making autonomy to policymakers in a democratic context. (I am avoiding here the obvious possibilities of an Orwellian 1984 by keeping the context overtly democratic, but these possibilities nevertheless should be kept in mind.) Boguslaw calls systems designers, engineers, city planners, some social scientists, operations researchers, and the computer boys in general the "new utopians," since they are working for a society in which all is uniform and human error is omitted. The new utopians are unique in that are concerned with "non-people and with people-substitutes," but not with "souls nor stomachs." People problems are not their bag.

As social complexities arise, the need for planned public policies will grow, and the new utopians will be the planners. Their expertise, their professionalism, their disinterest in people problems, will isolate them from democratic considerations in the designing of public policy. Politicians, in turn, will use the educated expertise of their professional planners as a lever for or as a defense against change: What the experts say is right must in fact be right because they are the experts. Information is the basis of expertise, and control of information technology should yield the controllers more expertise (i.e., arguments that can be marshalled in favor of policies preferred by the controllers) than they have ever enjoyed in the past.

Nevertheless, information technology also has tremendous potential for making government more responsive to social crises, but in a sense that connotes participatory democracy only indirectly. It gives policymakers the knowledge they need before they can apply solutions. This relates to James D. Caroll's notion of noetic authority. Information technology should make noetic politics, that is, policy decisions based on distributions of social and factual knowledge rather than on avaricious deals between interest groups, a far more feasible proposition than it is now. Policymakers can get the information they need for the problems with which they are confronted and in a considerably more parsimonious way. In this view, contentions for power will evolve from the politics of greed to the politics of knowledge. Who knows what will become more important than who has what. In brief, we may be entering a new era of politics, one that places greater stock in how knowledge and expertise are distributed in society, and lesser stock in how wealth is distributed than is the case now. With both, of course, we are still talking about the authoritative allocation of values, and who has the power to allocate values, but the principal currencies have changed, or at least, they may change.

There are overtones of benevolent despotism to noetic politics that are unavoidable, as Buguslaw has pointed out in terms of new utopianism. The essential difference between new utopianism and noetic authority, however, is one of people-problem sensitivity. With the former we are confronted with an engineering mentality at the helm. With the latter we are captained by a social scientist. In both, we are concerned with governance by officially certified experts in an increasingly complex society, "the public interest" defined as the systems approach, and the denigration of democratic values in favor of elitist values.

INFORMATION TECHNOLOGY AND MAN'S SELF-IMAGE

Communications theorist Marshall McLuhan contends that a single technological innovation is responsible for modern man: movable type. Right or wrong, there is something to be said for the impact of information technologies on all of us. Man's ability to state and record ideas is as unique to the species as the opposing thumb.

The acceptance and adoption of new information technologies in the last few years conjoins with larger technological developments that have immense implications for man's view of his world and himself. When Victor C. Ferkiss speaks of "technological man," he is referring to an astronaut-like strain of Homo sapiens that is qualitatively different from industrial man, who is a crushed member of the proletariat at worst and a Babbitt at best. Technological man is in control of his emotions, integrated into a man-machine-biosphere system (no longer an interface), and is the epitome of homeostasis. Information technology is central to the concept of technological man. For instance, John Rader Platt's "ultra-microuniversalium" is a technological extension of man's limited biological cerebrum.

Those analysts who embrance neopublishing techniques as an indispensable part of the welcome technological revolution share a modified Marxian view of the dialectic. In very gross terms, technology rather than industry will supply the material foundation for a new society. While not necessarily communal, the new society should be characterized by a new kind of freedom: physical wants will be supplied, psychological stress will be reduced, and human creativity will flourish. Information technology will play a major role in the latter two aspects of the new society. Data technology should reduce emotional stress by limiting the need for personal decision making (particularly those decisions that entail credit for blame for the decisionmaker), and it will foster humanistic creativity via its vast educational potential.

The revolutionary qualities innate to data technology in terms of education (life-long, self-directed, noninstitutional learning) have been discussed. Personal decision making, however, is another matter. Organization theorists have noted the propensity of participants in organizations to reduce uncertainty whenever possible. The "satisfying" decision is favored over the "maximizing" decision, the "programmed" decision over the "nonprogrammed" decision, and the routine over the unexpected. Such is the dynamic of Gresham's Law. Very few people relish making a decision when it entails personal risk, when a wrong move could bring blame. John Kenneth Galbraith's observation on the existence of a technostructure in American society that diffuses rather than focusses criticism and accountability, attests to the presence of an anti-decision-making bias in our culture that has erected very real and widespread defenses.

Computers can help those of us who are disinclined toward bureaucratic risk taking. They can make decisions for us. The only humans conceivably open to blame for incorrect choices would be computer programmers, although even they would be only remotely responsible.

Management scientist Herbert A. Simon has noted that machines in organizations have taken over the solving of "well-structured problems" and are working toward a take-over of "ill-structured problems" and the supervision of employees. This phenomenon has permitted more occupations that center around face-to-face interaction of people, which Simon considers more humanistic and gratifying. But computerized decision making also eliminates certain kinds of jobs that give a sense of self-worth to the job holder. Clerks and accountants are on the way out, and the increasingly heuristic problem-solving capacities of computers bode ill for middle management and even top executives. Simon welcomes such developments.

Boguslaw does not. While men may not enjoy the psychological dissonance created by decision making, they do need the status and self-esteem that recognition of their abilities and responsibilities brings. In this vein, Boguslaw speculates on the computer's implications for the Protestant ethic: "Will the unspoken creed, which once could be verbalized as 'I may not be a brain but I can always make a living with these hands; I am fundamentally the producer,' be replaced by another, which when verbalized might say, 'All these hands (or all this mind) can do is what some machine hasn't yet gotten around to doing.'"

Simon and Boguslaw are sufficiently representative of the two poles of the computer-technology-humanism-organization-management debate. What is worth examining further at this juncture are the potential effects of the new technologies on the managerial echelons of organizations, and there are a few studies that have attempted to do this. In them, the investigation missions of the authors revolve around such questions as: Will middle management be displaced by machines? Will top management control all variables in the organization via computer technologies and management science, or will it, too, be displaced by automation? Will administrators generally be alienated by the new machinery, or will they become true believers? Will the authority relationships and controlling abilities of administrators be altered by the use of computers? It is these kinds of concerns that characterize the studies that we shall review briefly in terms of the computer's impact on authority and control, organizational structure, and dehumanization and alienation.

A frequent premise of investigators is that computers facilitate the concentration and centralization of authority in organizations. Although empirical findings are mixed in this area, the bulk of the research tends to support the proposition but with some interesting variations. A study by Thomas L. Whisler of twenty-three large insurance companies indicated that where computers were introduced in the organization, decision-making loci tended to move upward in the hierarchy: Indeed, the most commonly reported phenomenon in the study was the centralizing of control after the introduction of computers. Computers tended to displace clerks in the companies. It was estimated that without electronic data processing, the companies would have required a 60 percent increase in their clerical staff, only a 9 percent hike in supervisory personnel, and a mere 2 percent increase in managerial jobs. Simon's observation on the propensity of EDP to solve well-structured, ill-structured, and supervisory problems in an ascending order of rapidity and accuracy would seem to be substantiated by Whisler's research.

From another viewpoint, however, managers report a decentralization of authority attributable to computers, but only in the sense that managers are released from routine chores and are able to spend more time on authoritative decsion making. In a study of fifty state employment agencies (plus Puerto Rico, the Virgin Islands, and Washington, D.C.), S. R. Klatsky observed a "cascade effect" in terms of authority as a result of computers. Computers created a vacuum of activity at the lowest managerial levels by freeing these managers from many routine jobs. If top-level managers then <u>decided</u> to let their authority devolve after the introduction of EDP, the resulting new authority granted to each level of the hierarchy could be handled more effectively since computers had taken over routine tasks. Thus, computers, together with a decision by top management to decentralize their authority, created a cascade of authority to lower levels that increased the mission effectiveness of the organization generally.

The cascade effect relates to another study conducted by Donald R. Shaul of fifty-three middle managers and fourteen top manager in eight companies. Shaul found that after EDP had been adopted, 60 percent of the managers reported an increase in planning activities, a high percentage increased their directing activities, and a greater propensity by managers to relinquish certain kinds of authority was observed. Interestingly, two-thirds of the managers reported less need to bother with controlling subordinates because the computer kept an adequate check on misuse of budgetary funds and work time, while opportunities for engaging in coordination activities increased.

Withington observes in this regard the phenomenon of "flickering authority" in organizations enabled by the advent of EDP. Because the computer frees all managers from a phethora of mundane duties and furnishes them with information that they can use more potently than ever before, they have more time to develop their ideas and more information to substantiate them, and authority thus becomes more accessible to all managers. In Withington's words, "The effect is that the authority for originating and testing ideas for change 'flickers' within the management structure of the organization. He who has the idea is the one who temporarily has the authority to proceed with its analysis . . . "

If computers have an effect on the exercise of authority in organizations, they have an equal impact on hierarchical structure. Most analysts agree that EDP will pressure the hierarchical pyrimid to flatten, and this pressure would appear to be the result of increased organizational control enabled by computer technology. John Pfiffner and Robert Presthus, for instance, speak of the bureaucratic pyrimid evolving into a "bell" formation because of EDP and the related techniques of systems analysis.

Changes due to EDP in organizational structure present difficulties for public administrators. A study by Marshall W. Meyer, using data gathered from 254 state, country, and city finance departments and comptrollers' offices, found that tensions arose between superordinates inexpert in EDP and subordinates proficient in computer science, because electronic data processing requirements forced superordinates and subordinates to cooperate in ways not provided by the traditional bureaucratic structure. If the organization was able to adapt to the use of EDP, Meyer found, horizontal interaction increased and the normal vertical interaction of the closed model decreased; if the organization was too stultified to change, administrative pathologies quickly surfaced. In this light, Whisler noted a blurring of traditional line-staff distinctions in organizations as a result of EDP; staff members with computer skills gained new organizational prestige.

If clerks are the bureaucrats most often displaced by automation, those clerks who remain frequently find that their jobs become rigidly routinized, and occasionally they are transformed into key punch operators. Such, at least, was the conclusion of Albert A. Blum in a study of EDP and white collar workers. On the other hand, the promotion possibilities for those clerks remaining are about the same as they were prior to the introduction of EDP. And Whisler found that, while clerical responsibilities were not enlarged, salaries went up with the omcreased need for clerical precision.

Older bureaucrats occasionally experience a sense of alienation when EDP is introduced. Meyer's findings imply this, but a study by H. S. Rhee specifically noted the presence of conflict between older, bureaucratic-oriented personnel and younger, professional-oriented workers over the automation issue.

Generally, most investigators seem to agree that EDP does not affect top-level decisionmakers very much one way or another. Rodney H. Brady, after interviewing more than 100 top managers and examining in detail the decision-making process in more than a dozen large companies, concluded that the computer has not had much impact on decision-making at the top. On the other hand, EDP has speeded the overall decision-making process in organizations by making more information more available to top managers. Rhee found that the concern over a computer-oriented technocratic elite eventually displacing top administrators to be a view not shared by top administrators themselves. In fact, highest-level decisionmakers did not consider a technical background to be a prerequisite for their positions. Whisler reported that the organizational centralization accompanying the introduction of computers tended to increase the responsiveness and power of the topmost echelon, while Shaul concluded that middle managers, too, believed that their responsibilities and capabilities had increased after the advent of EDP. In fact, when one considers the findings of Brady, Whisler, and Shaul together, one infers that all officials of all administrative levels in the organizational hierarchy feel that their personal status rises after the switch to EDP. While not all studies support this conclusion, it is a significant counterargument to the dehumanization hypothesis.

Still, one wonders. There have been reports in business magazines of deskless offices in the presidential stratum of progressive multinational corporations. In these poshest of quarters, there are no desks, only chairs, lounges, and coffee tables. The underlying assumption is that the topmost corporate decisionmaker should be only that. He should do no more than listen, confer, and decide; he should be relieved of anything resembling paperwork. The brain is all. Similarly, the growing fetish of the clean desk refers to the propensity of top-level administrators to have no more than one sheet of paper on their desks at any one time, and betokens an emphasis on thought and decision making rather than on paper shuffling. The presidents of private foundations seem to favor this clean desk affectation. Continuing this line of thinking, a major company recently introduced a waterbed room for use by its top-level executives (presumably on a one-at-a-time basis). The idea is that an executive floats, meditates, and ultimately decides about the grand issues facing the company.

Do these developments reflect anything other than a desire to make the decision-making process more effective and, more probably, pretentious? It seems possible, at least, that top executives may be trying to manipulate their images in such a way as to distinguish their functions from the functions of the computer. The more unlike they are from the computer, the less paper they handle, and the more they "think," the more essential they become as human beings. This, of course, is only speculation. But the increasing obsequiousness displayed for the decision-making function in organizations may reflect a subliminal fear over the awesome, if as yet unrealized, cognitive powers of The Computer. In this light, it is worth noting that a survey taken by S. R. Lee several years ago indicated that 24 percent of the respondents with a college degree and 44 percent of those who had not completed high school thought of computers as being "the fearsome thinking machine."

This sense of alienation and isolation resulting from the introduction of computers in organizations may be intensified by the presence of information network terminals in the home of the future. As we noted, Kahn has observed the propensity of children to get fixated on the instructional computer, and Nie has warned of the "privatization" of life styles that may be engendered by the information utility. The highly personalized home terminal may become a much more interesting conversationalist than one's spouse or progeny. Already, in fact, studies have indicated that the average American child from three through sixteen years of age spends more of his waking hours watching television than attending school, and that televised programs and commercials can have a measurable effect on the behavior of children. Recently, a study was conducted by the Society for Rational Psychology in West Germany in which 184 viewers were paid to be deprived of their television sets for a period of months. During this span of time, child spanking, moodiness, wife beating, and extramarital affairs increased among the viewers, and interest in sex decreased. None of the viewers were able to deny himself television for more than five months, and, with the return of the tube, "normal" behavior was restored. As one psychologist of the Society put it, "the problem is that of addiction."

Another cultural factor that is subject to change from data technology is that of speed. Speed is what Alvin Toffler has in mind when he speaks of "future shock", i.e., "the shattering stress and disorientation that we induce in individuals by subjecting them to too much change in too short a time." Man can take only so many stimuli, and after a certain level is reached he begins shutting them out. The scramble to acquire information (i.e., knowledge that changes us) should be accelerated by information technologies. In a fundamentally competitive society, use of a more versatile technology is not a matter of choice, but a matter of necessity. Information users already have had to step up their rates of functioning to survive, and this phenomenon should intensify the disease of change.

New information technologies also have looming implications for the concept of personal identity. Toffler argues, somewhat indirectly, that individualism is enhanced in technological societies, and that information technology plays an especially large role in this enhancement. The demassification of society is possible through self-editing techniques, and he cites the rise of numerous art theaters with small seating capacities, little magazines, the underground press, demographic editions, and the corresponding decline of movie palaces and mass-circulation slicks as evidence.

Yet while the reader may write what he wishes to read on an increasingly wide and heterogeneous scale, the technology that allows him to do so is homogenizing. Neopublishing systems are blending photocopying, microreproduction, television, and computer techniques in preparation for the information networks of the future. Technology in general seems to be contributing to the homogenization of the global environment. As economist Kenneth Boulding has noted, "the tractor is much the same everywhere," and that this "imposes a uniformity at least on the technological culture of the world."

The environment, particularly the aesthetic environment, is a new and ill-understood issue. What _is_ man's relationship with his physical surroundings? It at least seems possible that technological man, in the holistic, ecological meaning Ferkiss gives him, will have attitudinal uniformity concerning his technological culture, partly as a result of technological uniformity itself. Information technology specifically may provide the sole means by which man may foster his own humanistic identity via self-editing techniques, despite the overt homogeneity of a technological era.

Such an ability, which should become increasingly critical to man's understanding of himself in a machine dominated world, also should increase man's own role conflict. With every man his own publisher, editor, writer, teacher, reader, and researcher, these heretofore distinct identities (which themselves have been spawned by technology) may become confused. This confusion of roles could have implications for art itself, as author and publisher William Jovanovich suggests:

> What if everyone did actually write his story, and what if everyone's story were Xeroxed? Imagine millions and millions of welterweight Norman Mailers, each making himself the center of existence and each describing his feelings as the only trustworthy view of the world's ways. Imagine it! What would all that writing, the whole of it, amount to? It might be life. It might be what no artist can conceive, bigger than the biggest vision of poets and madmen. That's it. That's what the Universal Xerox Life Compiler Machine could do for us, something "now" and "total," so to speak.

Jovanovich's notion of some immense pattern of humanity's ideas, "bigger than the biggest visions of poets and madmen," and all of it produced by those contraptions we find in libraries, ties in with more serious conceptualizations concerning man's destiny. Philosopher Pierre Teilhard de Chardin's idea of the moosphere, the sum totality of human thought encompassing the earth, is a mystical dialectic that perceives man progressing toward a conquest of boredom, a victory of rationality, and a release from being the children of a paternalistic God. In less theological terms, Boulding sees this progression as "the meaning of the twentieth century." Science is the basis of "the great transition" now occurring, but what is unique to our age is that knowledge no longer is a depreciable commodity. It can be stored and retrieved at will, thus giving men more time to acquire new information rather than preserving and transmitting it. Boulding combines Teilhard's moosphere, Professor Derek J. de Solla Price's more tangible concept of the invisible college of highest-quality scientists, and the reality of information technology to predict a postcivilization dominated by survival-oriented rationality. It would be the fulfillment of information technology's potential or, in biologist Platt's words, "a memory and the beginnings of a universal brain for the whole human race."

If this sounds utopian, it is. Utopia, that is, the use of knowledge to eliminate want (and possibly challenge) and assure survival, may be the only society possible in the technological earth of the future. Noetic politics may be the politics of necessity in a society more interconnected and complex than anything we ever have imagined. It is time for public policymakers to face up to that necessity.

REFERENCES

Armer, Paul (1970). Computer applications in government. In The computer impact, Irene Taviss (Ed.), Englewood Cliffs, New Jersey: Prentice-Hall, Inc.

Arthur D. Little, Inc. (1966). The impact of technology on publishing. In An economic-media study of book publishing, New York: The American Textbook Publishers Institute and the American Book Publishers Council, 119-163.

Beer, Stafford (1970). Managing modern complexity. In The management of information and knowledge. A compilation of papers prepared for the Eleventh Meeting of the Panel on Science and Technology, Committee on Science and Astronautics, U.S. House of Representatives. Washington: U.S. Government Printing Office, 41-62.

Bengeldorf, Irving S. (1970). The Information Utility and Social Change. In The information utility and social choice. Harold Sackman and Norman Nie (Eds.). Monvale, New Jersey: AFIPS Press, 167-181.

Bernstein, Mavor (1955). Regulating business by independent commissions. Princeton, New Jersey. Princeton University Press.

Blaisdell, William M. (1960). Study no. 2: Size of the copyright industries. In Copyright Law Revision. Studies prepared for the Subcommittee on Patents, Trademarks, and Copyrights of the Committee on the Judiciary, United States Senate, 86yh Cong., 1st Sess., May 1959. Pursuant to S. Res. 53. Studies 1-4. Washington: U.S. Government Printing Office, 21-59.

Blum, Albert A. (1970). White collar workers. In The Computer Impact, Irene Taviss (Ed.). Englewood Cliffs, New Jersey: Prentice-Hall, Inc., 69-80.

Boguslaw, Robert (1965). The New Utopians: A study of systems design and social change. Englewood Cliffs, New Jersey: Prentice-Hall, Inc.

Boulding, Kenneth (1964). The meaning of the twentieth century: The great transition. New York: Harper and Row, Publishers.

Brady, Rodney H. (1967). Computers in top-level decision making. Harvard Business Review Vol. 45, July-August, 67-76.

Brudner, Harvey J. (1968). Computer-managed instruction. Science 162, November 29, 970-976.

Caffrey, John and Mosmann, Charles J. (1967). Computers on campus. A report to the President on their use and management. Washington: American Council on Education.

Carroll, James D. (1969). Noetic authority. Public Administration Review XXIX, September-October, 492-500.

Cary is new copyright mead: Ringer sues, charging bias (1971). Publishers' Weekly CC, September 6, p. 29.

Clark, Burton R. (1965). Inter-organizational patterns in education. Administrative Science Quarterly X, September, 224-237.

Davis, Watson (1967). The universal brain: Is centralized storage and retrieval of all knowledge possible, feasible, or desirable? In The growth of knowledge: Readings on organization and retrieval of information. Manfred Kochen (Ed.). New York: John Wiley and Sons, Inc., 60-65.

de Chardin, Pierre Teilhard (1965). The phenomenon of man. New York: Harper and Row.

de Solla Price, Derek J. (1963). Little science, big science. New York: Columbia University Press.

Dordick, H. S. (1968). The new communication technology and for what? Santa Monica, California: The RAND Corporation, May.

Edelman, Murray (1964). The symbolic uses of politics. Urabana, Illinois: University of Illinois Press.

Editors of Scientific American information (1965). A Scientific American Book. San Francisco: W. H. Freeman.

Etzioni, Amitai (1969). Project knowledge: Over-collecting and under-analyzing in the data industry. The Wall Street Journal, March 18, p. 16.

Ferkiss, Victor C. (1969). Technological man: The myth and the reality. New York: New American Library.

Galbraith, John Kenneth (1967). The new industrial state. Boston: Houghton Mifflin Co.

Garceau, Oliver (1958). Interest group theory in political research. Annals of the American Academy of Political and Social Science CCCXIX, September, 104-112.

Greenberger, Martin (Ed.) (1971). Computers, communications, and the public interest. Baltimore, Maryland: The Johns Hopkins Press.

Herring, E. Pendleton (1936). Public administration and the public interest. New York: McGraw-Hill.

Johnson, David L. and Kobler, Author L. (1962). The man-computer relationship. Science 138, November 23, 873-879.

Jovanovich, William (1971). The universal Xerox Life Compiler Machine. The American Scholar XL, Spring, 249-255.

Kahn, Herman (1970). The 'Emergent United States' . . . post-industrial society. The Management of Information and Knowledge. A compilation of papers prepared for the Eleventh Meeting of the Panel on Science and Technology, Committee on Science and Astronautics, U.S. House of Representatives. Washington: U.S. Government Printing Office, 17-40.

Kaminstein, Abraham L. (1964). Transcript of meeting, January 15, 1964. In Copyright law revision. Part 4. Further discussions and comments on preliminary draft for revised U.S. copyright law. 88th Cong., 2nd Sess. December, 1964. Washington: U.S. Government Printing Office, 229.

Kanter, J. (1967). The computer and the Executive. Englewood Cliffs, N.J.: Prentice-Hall.

Katz, Aaron (1964). Toward high information level culture. Cybernetica VII, No. 3, 203-245.

Klatzky, S. R. (1970). Automation, size, and the locus of decision making: The cascade effect. The Journal of Business Vol. 43, April, 141-151.

Kochen, Manfred (Ed.) (1967). The growth of knowledge: Readings on organization and retrieval of information. New York: John Wiley and Sons, Inc.

Kohlmeier, Louis M., Jr. (1969). The regulators: Watchdog agencies and the public interest. New York: Harper and Row, Publishers.

Kong, S. L. (1968). Education in the cybernetic age: A model. Phi Delta Kappan XLIX, October, 71-74.

Lakoff, Sanford A. (Ed.) (1966). Knowledge and power: Essays on science and government. New York: The Free Press.

Lamberton, D. M. (Ed.) (1971). Economics of information and knowledge: Selected readings. Middlesex: Penguin Books.

Lane, Robert E. (1966). The decline of politics and ideology in a knowledgeable society. American Sociological Review XXXI, October, 649-662.

Lee, R. S. "Social Attitudes and the Technological Revolution." Unpublished manuscript.

Leonard, E. et al. (1971). MINERVA: A participatory technology system. Bulletin of the Atomic Scientists XXVII, November, 4-12.

Licklider, J. C. R. (1965). Libraries of the future. Cambridge, Massachusetts: M.I.T. Press.

Markham, Jesse W. (1966). An economic analysis of the new information technologies. In An economic-media study of book publishing. New York: The American Textbook Publishers Institute and the American Book Publishers Council, 1-27.

McLuhan, Marshall (1962). The Gutenberg galaxy: The making of typographic man. Toronto: University of Toronto Press.

Meyer, Marshall W. (1968). Automation and bureaucratic structure. American Journal of Sociology Vol. 74, November, 256-264.

Meynand, Jean (1968). Technocracy. London: Faber and Faber.

Michael, Donald N. (1968). On coping with complexity: Planning and politics. Daedalus XCVII, Fall, 1179-1193.

Miller, Arthur R. (1971). The assault on privacy: Computers, data banks, and dossiers. Ann Arbor, Michigan: University of Michigan Press.

Nie, Norman H. (1970). Future developments in mass communications and citizen participation. In The information utility and social choice, Harold Sackman and Norman Nie (Eds.). Montvale, New Jersey: AFIPS Press.

Oettinger, Anthony G. with Marks, Sema (1969). Run, computer run: The mythology of educational innovation. Cambridge, Massachusetts: Harvard University Press.

Parker, Edwin B. and Dunn, Donald A. (1972). Information technology: Its social potential. Science CLXXVI, June 30, 1392-1399.

Platt, John Rader (1966). The step to man. New York: John Wiley and Sons, Inc., p. 216.

Redford, Emmett M. (1952). Administration of national economic control. New York: Macmillan.

Reich, Charles A. (1970). Without Marx or Jesus, the new American Revolution has begun. Translated from the French by Bernard Jack. New York: Doubleday.

Rhee, H. A. (1968). Office automation in social perspective. Oxford: Basil Blackwell.

Roszak, Theodore J. (1969). The making of a counterculture: Reflections on the technocratic society and its youthful opposition. New York: Doubleday.

Schattschneider, E. E. (1935). Politics, pressure and the tariff: A study of free private enterprise in pressure politics, as shown in the 1929-1930 revision of the tariff. New York: Prentice-Hall, Inc.

Schmandt, Juergen (1970). Technology and education. In Issues in American education: Commentary on the current scene, Arthur M. Kroll (Ed.). New York: Oxford University Press, 78-86.

Shaul, Donald R. (1964). What's really ahead for middle management. Personnel 41, November-December, 9-16.

Simon, Herbert A. (1965). The shape of automation for men and management. New York: Harper and Row.

Smith, Roger H. (1964). Copyright revision and the library of the future. Publishers' Weekly CLXXXV, May 11, p. 36.

Tarkelson, Gerald M. and Tarkelson, Emily A. (1967). How mechanized should the classroom be? NEA Journal CCCLXVIII, March, 28-30.

Taviss, Irene and Burbank, Judith (Eds.) (1971). Implications of computer technology: Research review 7. Cambridge, Massachusetts: Harvard University Program on Technology and Society.

Toffler, Alvin (1970). Future shock. New York: Random House.

Tyler, Ralph W. (1965). The knowledge explosion: Implications for secondary education. The Educational Forum XXIX, January, 145-153.

Wagner, Susan (1971). Barbara Ringer endorsed by former copyrignt chief. Publishers' Weekly CC, October 18, p. 30.

Wagner, Susan (1971). Carey renamed Register of Copyrights. Publishers' Weekly CC, November 8, p. 29.

Wagner, Susan (1971). New Register of Copyrights expected this year. Publishers' Weekly CXCIC, January 18, p. 35.

Warthman, Forrest (1974). Telecommunication and the city." The Annals of the American Academy of Political and Social Science, "The Information Revolution," Donald M. Lamberton (Special Ed.) 412, March, 127-137.

Westin, Alan F. (1970). Information systems and political decision-making. In The Computer Impact, Irene Taviss (Ed.). Englewood Cliffs, New Jersey: Prentice-Hall, Inc., 130-144.

Westin, Alan F. (Ed.) (1971). Information technology in a democracy. Harvard Series on Technology and Society. Cambridge, Massachusetts: Harvard University Press.

Westin, Alan F. (1967). Privacy and freedom. New York: Atheneum.

Whisler, Thomas L. (1970). The impact of computers on organizations. New York: Praeger Publishers.

Wiener, Norbert (1954). The human use of human beings: Cybernetics and society. New York: Doubleday.

Withington, Frederic G. (1969). The real computer: Its influence, uses, and effects. Reading, Mass.: Addison-Wesley Pub. Co.

INDEX

*Underlined numbers give the page on which the complete reference is listed.